Breakout

Breakout: Pilgrim in the Microworld

David Sudnow

Boss Fight Books
Los Angeles, CA
bossfightbooks.com

ISBN-13: 978-1-940535-23-4
Originally published by Warner Books, Inc. in 1983 under the title
Pilgrim in the Microworld: Eye, Mind and the Essence of Video Skill

First Boss Fight Books Printing: 2019

Series Editor: Gabe Durham
Associate Editor: Michael P. Williams
Book Design by Cory Schmitz
Page Design by Christopher Moyer

For Paul, Jessica, Larry, and Danny

With the fearful prayer that the only ICBMs they ever encounter are the Atari sort.

CONTENTS

FOREWORD

A FEW YEARS AGO at an indie games festival I got coffee with the Australian games scholar and writer Brendan Keogh, who at the time was probably best known for his book *Killing is Harmless*, a scene-by-scene exploration of the military shooter *Spec Ops: The Line*.

I mentioned that I'd been glad to see his meditation on a single video game come out to public enthusiasm just as I was launching a press for this very kind of book. "You got there before anybody," I said.

"Not quite anybody," Keogh said. "Have you heard of *Pilgrim in the Microworld*?"

Pilgrim, he told me, was a critical and personal deep dive into the Atari game *Breakout*—a kind of field report from inside the author's own obsession. It was published in 1983, a Boss Fight book long before Boss Fight Books existed. Before *I* existed, for that matter.

I sought out a copy of *Pilgrim* in its original hardback, which features an awesomely dated cover: A human eye stares out at the reader as *Tron*-y vectors and green fireworks pop out in all directions. But the text inside the book was much harder to pin down to its decade.

Sudnow's fascination with video games begins as he watches his son play *Missile Command* in a dark arcade, and he quickly begins to anthropologize these young people. Soon enough at a party, he observes his own peers—professors no less!—preferring the thrills of *Breakout* on a home console over the respectable pastimes of singing jazz standards around the piano. As the author begins to try to master the game as he would a musical instrument, Sudnow starts to (charmingly, self-awarely) go a little crazy. As in the best nonfiction, Sudnow lends his subject a roving authorial eye that takes in—and questions—everything.

I was intrigued. Who was this Sudnow guy? And didn't he know that that all games writing from before 2004 is legally required to suck?

•

Breakout's creation story lies at the intersection of three tech titans: Atari founder Nolan Bushnell, and the eventual Apple Computers founders Steve Jobs and Steve Wozniak.

Atari's game *Pong* was the first-ever multi-platinum video game smash hit, and *Breakout* came from an idea of Bushnell's while Atari was looking for its Next Big Thing: What if there was a one-player version of *Pong*?

Where you control a single paddle at the bottom of the screen, knocking the Pong ball into a wall of bricks at the top of the screen, destroying the wall brick by brick?

Bushnell put nineteen-year-old Jobs in charge of programming the game with the challenge of designing it using as few chips as possible. Fewer chips meant huge savings for Atari, and Bushnell offered bonuses to game developers who could keep costs down.

Not much of a programmer, Jobs brought in his brilliant best friend, Wozniak, to design the game. Wozniak's design of *Breakout* was so tightly constructed that Atari had to add *more* chips to the circuit board just to create a version that the engineers at Atari understood well enough to reproduce. Still, Bushnell paid a large bonus to Jobs to split with Wozniak (either $5,000 or $30,000 depending on your source). Jobs instead lied to Wozniak about how much the bonus was, gave Wozniak just $375, and pocketed the rest.

The experience taught Wozniak a lot about his partner. "He told me he was giving me 50 percent," Wozniak said. "I knew he believed that it was fine to buy something for $60 and sell it for $6,000 if you could do it. I just didn't think he would do it to his best friend." Jobs went on to make the exploitation of brilliant colleagues one of the hallmarks of his career. And Wozniak never made another game again.

•

But *Breakout* is not simply a historical footnote in the lives of powerful men. It's a genuine classic that has spawned many sequels and imitators since its 1976 arcade release. The Atari 2600 version was one of the first games to be released for Atari's first and best-known console—it was this version Sudnow played while writing *Pilgrim*. There are the game's direct sequels, such as *Super Breakout*, *Breakout 2000*, and *Breakout Boost*.

Then there's Taito's popular 1986 arcade game *Arkanoid*, which improved on *Breakout*'s formula with improved graphics, power-ups, level variety, and different types of bricks. *Arkanoid* itself was popular enough to warrant several sequels including *Revenge of Doh* and *Arkanoid: Doh it Again*.

And then there's *Alleyway*, which I was surprised to discover was created by Nintendo's famed R&D1 branch. One of only five launch titles when Game Boy debuted in Japan in 1989, *Alleyway* appears to be directly modeled on *Arkanoid*, from the level design to your paddle's "space capsule" look. (Although a close look at the game's box art reveals that in this *Breakout* clone, your paddle is being operated by a potbellied plumber who's never met a cameo he didn't like.) But without *Arkanoid*'s power-up system, *Alleyway* was a bit of a disappointment—a faded copy of a copy.

Breakout's influence extends far beyond obvious clones. Tomohiro Nishikado, hooked on the game when he began designing *Space Invaders*, loved the way the ball speeds up and how levels only move on when you've cleared the screen—and he set out to create something even better. "Using *Breakout* as a base, my first, rough idea was to use the blocks in a different way, for some kind of shooting game." *Space Invaders* was so popular that it not only inspired its own genre (what we sometimes call the "gallery shooter"), it's also credited by Nintendo's Shigeru Miyamoto as the game whose popularity convinced him there might just be a career for him in video games. From there, the tree of influence branches off in a thousand different directions.

Luckily for the game's preservation, Atari makes sure that each of their classics from the company's Golden Age is collected and re-released with the advent of each new console generation. The PS4 release of *Atari Flashback Classics: Volume 2*, for instance, features *three* different versions of *Breakout* (just in case you feel the need to compare the arcade version of *Super Breakout* to the 2600 version). Just like *Pong*, *Asteroids*, *Missile Command*, *Centipede*, and *Space Invaders*, *Breakout* is now too deeply ingrained into the History of Gaming to ever really go away.

•

I mention all the backstory above because you're not going to see it in the book itself. David Sudnow didn't much care about where Breakout came from, who came up with it, or what the game's enduring legacy would be.

Pilgrim was instead written from a place of obsession. This was not an unusual starting point for Sudnow. As his widow, Wendy Lu, told me on the phone, "He was the type of person where when he gets into something, he's all-in." He had a tendency to get into a new hobby, art form, or field of study, and would enjoy becoming consumed by it.

In a chapter where Sudnow pays a visit to Atari's offices, Sudnow does not fanboy out over meeting the programmers who worked on his favorite game. Sudnow writes, upon meeting a programmer, "If anybody could tell me how to play the game, he could." And then proceeds to hit the programmer up for tips.

Lu describes Sudnow's daily routine as very consistent. Every morning he was up at five o'clock, he'd read the news, and then he'd start writing about whatever he wanted.

"So by that point in his life," I said, "he'd really cultivated a lot of discipline, then?"

"I wouldn't call him disciplined, exactly," she said. "He felt *compelled* to write. He couldn't help it."

•

Sudnow was born in the Bronx to a family of music lovers. His grandfather had a music career in Russia before immigrating to the US amidst political turmoil. Sudnow's father was a pianist, but became a pharmacist out of a desire to be practical.

Sudnow's own career vacillated between more practical work in academia and the love of music that he shared with his father and grandfather. Sudnow studied at University of Alabama, went to UC Berkeley for his PhD in sociology, and eventually became the youngest tenured professor at UC Irvine. While in graduate school, Sudnow fell in with a slightly fringy philosophical offshoot of sociology called ethnomethodology. Though I had to sift through a lot of confusing academic jargon to understand it, ethnomethodology is just the study of how people act in social situations—it seeks to observe and pick apart all the social mores we typically take for granted.

For instance, Harold Garfinkel (coiner of the term "ethnomethodology") gives this example: A guy asks his friend how he's doing. Instead of saying "fine," the friend goes, "How am I in regard to what? My health, my finance, my school work, my peace of mind, my—" until the first guy loses it. "Look!" he screams. "I was just trying to be polite. Frankly, I don't give a damn how you are." The fact that the guy threw a fit just because his friend failed to follow a small social convention shows just how powerful that convention is. *Just say you're fine. Everybody knows you're supposed to just say you're fine.*

This background explains a lot about Sudnow's approach—for how detailedly he records the game and himself in conversation with one another. In *Pilgrim*, we see Sudnow turn his focus on the subtle mechanics that make the game harder and more complex than it initially appears—how each of your paddle's five invisible quadrants affects the angle of the ball, the way the ball suddenly speeds up on its eighth bounce—and how understanding those mechanics might make him a master… if only his hands would cooperate.

As much as the book is about *Breakout*, *Pilgrim* is about Sudnow himself. Specifically, it's about the challenges of being a person in a body who intellectually knows what he must do to clear the screen, but—like a piano student learning, say, "Moonlight Sonata"—must fail again and again, even as others make it look so easy.

Pilgrim has the most in common with Sudnow's 1978 book about how he learned to play jazz piano, *Ways of the Hand*, for which he was awarded a Guggenheim Fellowship. (Marvin Minsky's blurb for the *Pilgrim*'s original printing even goes so far as to frame *Pilgrim* as a "worthy sequel" to *Ways*.) *Ways* explores how the learning of piano is as much about the hands teaching themselves through what we now call "muscle memory" as it is about the conscious mind. His philosophy led to the creation of the "Sudnow Method" of learning piano, which emphasizes getting to the good stuff immediately by learning songs on day one, always beginning with the jazz standard "Misty."

Eventually, Sudnow's piano work eclipsed his sociology work—or maybe you could say his interests merged. He toured constantly to teach piano. Went on TV a lot. The host of NPR's *All Things Considered*, Robert Conley, took up piano as an adult and studied under Sudnow. When the internet became The Internet, Sudnow set up the Sudnow Method online, and personally managed the comments forum.

Even with his webmaster duties, he was still traveling and teaching, with newspaper ads for his seminars claiming that over 27,000 students had become better pianists thanks to the Sudnow Method. The program was a success. "Somewhere, somebody should be able to unlock the formula," *The Today Show* once raved, "and David did it." Of course, by then Sudnow had already unlocked a formula for longform video game criticism that would take decades to become common practice. The formula is simple: You give the game the respect of your full attention.

•

When *Pilgrim* was released, reviewers were passionately divided.

The *San Francisco Chronicle* called it "exhilarating… whether or not you have ever played a video game." *Kirkus Reviews* called it "an engaging personal experience with just enough social commentary to reassure parents that all those quarters may not be lost in vain." And *Booklist* called it "brilliant… a most serious study, portending the inevitable changes in the way we view our world."

But it's the book's pans that fascinate me—especially for what they can tell us about the world *Pilgrim* was born into.

The *Philadelphia Inquirer*'s John Marchese summarily dismissed *Pilgrim*'s premise, saying the book "proves what most readers already know: The games are more fun to play than to read about."

The Technology Review faults the book for not selecting a better, more complex game. "The microworld is indeed a compelling, possibly dangerous, undeniably important land, and a pilgrimage may be in order," writes Joseph A. Menosky. "But there is little to be said for a pilgrim who stumbles across a rock and mistakes it for a temple."

Writing for *Library Journal*, Norman Sondak of San Diego State University calls the book "a rambling, idiosyncratic apologia for [Sudnow's] descent into video game madness." If that sounds as exciting to you as it does to me, understand that the reviewer meant it as an insult.

The *News Journal* of Wilmington, Delaware, got violent. "Some editor at Warner Books should have slapped this 'microathlete' up the side of his head," wrote Gary Soulsman, anticipating the prose style of YouTube commenters decades ahead of his time.

For our best hope at a balanced review, we turn to Robert Gardner in the *New York Times*. And indeed, Gardner's review gamely praises and criticizes the book on its own merits from several different lenses until, sadly, Gardner tips his hand in the final sentence: "[Sudnow's] book, unfortunately, is tied to the intrinsic interest of video games, which figure to go the way of the hula hoop, Rubik's Cube, and the pinball machine." Aha! The lurking question finally reveals itself: Why would anyone dedicate so much attention to such a silly fad?

•

Video games, it turns out, have not gone away. (For that matter, neither have pinball machines or Rubik's cubes, and even hula hoops have their defenders.)

And over the years, game historians, journalists, and fans have rediscovered the book one by one and then passed it on to new pilgrims like a secret. In contemporary discussions of *Pilgrim*, the question that comes up again and again is not "Why would anyone write this?" but instead "Why has it taken critics so long to employ the kind of experiential (or, if you prefer, *phenomenological*) games writing that Sudnow was doing decades ago?" As Anna Anthropy wrote in 2011, "We're still struggling to convince games journalists to do what David Sudnow was doing in 1983."

"[*Pilgrim* is] relevant not only as a historic and early piece of video game criticism," Brendan Keough wrote in 2014, "but as something that touches on many of the themes that the current wave of games criticism, self included, only now are starting to rediscover."

I wonder if Sudnow felt vindicated watching the rise of gaming (and, much slower, the rise of games criticism) until his death in 2007. Or maybe after finally getting his fill of *Breakout*, he left gaming behind entirely, already eagerly moving on to the next obsession. Wendy Lu told me that David was proud of the book, and that he'd have been delighted to see it inspiring the next generation of writers more than three decades later.

But even as Sudnow's approach influences others, it's his prose style that elevates the book from a dry academic treatise to a truly alive work of creative nonfiction. Sudnow-the-narrator is punny, silly, full of cute turns of phrase and dad jokes. The whole book is suffused with a prankster's energy, the joy of trying to get away with something. Even as the author is endlessly frustrated in scene after scene with his own lack of competence with a 2600 controller, Sudnow often seems delighted on the page to be making use of a skill that he's already been practicing for most of his life—the skill of a writer.

The *News Journal* reviewer wrote that "[Sudnow] assumes we will be fascinated even when he starts to wander verbally"—but I don't think that's entirely correct. I think Sudnow is barely considering us at all.

Like so many books that I love, *Pilgrim* reads as if it was not written with an audience in mind but rather because the author has stuff he needs to work out on the page. As Jon Irwin puts it in a 2013 Kill Screen article, "Sudnow's is the journal of a man trapped at sea, writing for an audience of one." And with that skill comes freedom and confidence. There's no visible shame or self-reproach for diving so deep into this obsession. Because this game has consumed him so completely, there must be value to be mined from reporting from inside the obsession.

Today, as in 1983, whether or not you're on board with Sudnow's book has everything to do with how much respect you have for both Sudnow's subject and his mission. In this way, the book's strengths and its excesses are inextricable from one another. It's verbose. It's singularly focused. It doesn't waste time trying to coerce you. It's messy and human. It's pure experiential games writing heroin.

Every year, as gaming grows as both an art form and an industry, and as understanding the odd sway games hold over us becomes more and more essential to understanding *us*, the more clearly we can see how confined our conversations about gaming have been—and how instrumental Sudnow is in showing us how to break out.

Gabe Durham
Fall, 2019

MEMORY

I FIRST WENT INTO A VIDEO ARCADE to retrieve my teenager. The semester was over, I was in the Renaissance Cafe a block from campus grading final papers, and he was upstairs at the Superball Arcade. "Just a couple of quarters, Dad, please." Enough for me to have my coffee in peace. An hour later I'm ready to go. What's he doing up there? You could hear explosions muffle through the ceiling, and walking upstairs was like coming upon a contest between a rock band and a mortar battalion. How can they stand the megatones? How do ears adjust? Does the loudness decrease or the rest of the world just get quiet? The composer John Cage put himself in one of those research chambers devoid of all sound. He nonetheless began to hear two tones, one very low, the other high, and was told the first was his blood circulating and the second his nervous system. Now a reverse milieu, our new electric brain sets turned up to the maximum and the only quiet left to imagination.

When you first enter one of these places, not the shopping plaza sort with carpets, old fashioned lighting, a more polite volume, and parents holding little kids up to reach the controls, but inner-city versions where the heavies hang out, you know you're in a new species of public place. Strangers of all kinds pack in tight along the walls, intensely engrossed in private behavior while browsers come close up from behind to watch. Rear ends are dark and faces flicker. Something vital is being dispensed

He was still on his first quarter at a game called *Missile Command*, and when I put my hand on his shoulder it was like touching a statue. "Come on, Paul. Let's go." *Wang, wang, wang, wang … bang.* "Paul, I said let's go." "I got six cities in memory," he snapped between volleys as the score racked up to 120,000. "Well, you'll just have to forget them because I want to get out of here." I don't think he heard me, so I stood off and watched him play, or whatever you could say he was doing. If "doing" was the right word. Maybe the point was just to have your part in creating the noise? I couldn't make heads or tails of what was happening so I took a quarter and dropped it into the next machine over. Same game. Do they consider how to divide up the room? *Missile Command* and *Defender* in the northeast corner, *Centipede* and *Frogger* in the south, *Berzerk* to the West, and cartoon types near the entrance so the scene doesn't look too ominous should concerned parents peek in.

Without reading the instructions on the machine, for how could you listen in such noise, I put in my coin and all hell of one form or another broke loose. Then, with no sense I was playing a game, not knowing who "I" was among the various moving objects on screen, not even sure "I" was there—without the slightest idea whether, why, or when whatever was happening would end, it was all over. It even told me: THE END. What gall. I glanced at the instructions. Minimalist understatements. Enough to make sure you know to put in money. Some business this coin-op irony. Make the widespread confusion about what's worth paying for explicit: Spend your dough in order to appreciate the absurdity of getting nothing in return. I tried another game and before I knew it, again, the thing told me: GAME OVER. "Told me?"

Well, there were kids standing all around, and whenever I'd get to a machine one would soon enough show up and put a quarter by the slot along the overhead rack of the console, house etiquette for reserving rights to the next quartered round. I was happy to be bailed out of the foolishness, not about to pay to stand there looking like an idiot. At least in casinos you can fake what little you need by following the bets of someone who looks competent. The casino was the closest thing I could think of, for when you really got down to it, in both instances the prize seemed to be just holding on. Their looks looked that way.

The kid was still accumulating cities in memory, whose or which kind I couldn't say, least of all why, and by now a few others were standing over his shoulders to watch. As I headed his way I flashed on a poolroom in the Bronx. I'm in the midst of running three straight racks on my favorite table in the back corner, and a couple of kids are watching, when my father comes in. He never liked me hanging out there, but allowed it within limits. Caught between hoping he'd come close enough to see me do my thing and wishing he'd leave so I could keep it sacred, I freeze up. Now here I am, on the other side of the stage in that drama. I stood close enough to see his final score for myself, but not to where he'd see me see him. I watched and waited and waited but he kept holding on. How can you interrupt someone saving the world, let alone your own kid, but when I sensed this could go on for some time, I took the risk and browsed around, like window shopping at night with a Sony Walkman at peak volume between two very closely spaced rock stations.

Barooom, ICBMs hit MIRVs—"mirvs" as our kids say—sirens announce incoming enemy rounds much too fast for comfort, machine-gunning *rat tat tat tats* rack up the score, and then a little computerized melody, no bugle cry or Tchaikovsky overture but a piccolo-ranged bit of Schönbergian fluff, easy and cheap to program I suppose, joyfully signals you've won back an obliterated city.

Two adjacent machines. A kid, maybe ten at the most, stands right next to some preppy law school type at least twice his age. From my perspective they behave identically. Each body rivals the other as perfect specimens of the strangest human conduct I've witnessed in a public place. I see right hands putting epileptic seizures to shame, while the rest of them just stares and cares, standing up, watching TV.

Two adjacent machines. In one you apparently try to get a frog through four lanes of heavy traffic to reach the safety of a grassy divider, and if you don't use your legs right, you get a good simulated splat. When will they squirt at us? In the next one over on a black screen there's nothing but white Rorschach-shaped outlines moving around, and you're to hit them, so to speak, before they hit you. Once you've figured out what "you" is. The name on the machine implies you're in a field of asteroids, not that you know what a field of asteroids is, or what it'd be like to be a being in one. Here's where you learn. Now ask players at each game what's going on. One says you gotta get the frog to the other side. The other says you gotta keep from getting hit by asteroids. But the hands don't reveal the difference, twitching on for dear life.

Two adjacent machines. Spectacular little fantasy worlds, a moving connect-up-the-dots-to-get-through-the-maze-game. How utterly more spectacular if we didn't forget so fast. Another flashback, same time ago as before, my father and I on a plane from La Guardia to New Haven and back again, so I could feel flying. I'd taken a camera and was acutely disappointed when the pictures had come back a week later. The extraordinary sensations of that day were lost in a simulated view of mere things. Those are clouds. That's the tip of the plane. So much wanting a good souvenir of the experience, I'd ended up with a piece of glossy paper.

I remembered the sadness I felt on my first cross-Atlantic flight ten years later, when I noticed that only about three or four noses or even Nikons were pressed to the windows when the icebergs went by, or we went by the icebergs, whichever it is, I've forgotten. Everybody else either snoozed his way from one meal to the next or looked at pictures and listened to imaginary voices on paper, while icebergs were there, real honest to God icebergs like you've never seen before and you could moreover take pictures of them with your own two hands. Maybe some were reading about icebergs.

Watching this spectacular fantasy world under glass, whose marvels we'd as soon forget as we forget the "real" one, wondering how our new crystal memory box could possibly help us out of this endlessly spiraling amnesia, I was most struck by the opponent. Not just the tip of your pencil to contend with for connecting up the dots to get through the maze, but the tips of others as well, four others, intent on breaking your point. And you can't push their arms out of the way as with your kid brother in the backseat of the car. You just have to watch them carefully and move carefully, and they keep time very well, their kind, at your expense. One player seems to be connecting up, and the other can barely draw. From where I stand I can't tell if it's because the one doesn't watch as well or move as well or both. But this kid knows how to deal with the armless opponent and the other doesn't. Something vital is being dispensed, and know-how controls the dosage and cost. When they're both just as good, do they have precisely the same know-how, since the opponent is a machine? Can't tell from where I stand, but a specter of rigorously uniform training somehow hovers overhead.

I got back in time. Paul was still holding on. And several others were now watching, maybe five in all. Dead quiet but for the war. Yet from where I stood it looked like he was having a tough go at it, for his overall stance had tightened as though the fingers were getting through to him. And in about five minutes he missed whatever it was that finally matters, hit the machine, and said, "Damn." I moved in, rehearsing my praise, wondering what to say.

I thought of how you lie down in the hot sun, snuggling a groove in the sand to settle back into yourself, and with a deep sigh say, "Wow, isn't this wonderful." That "wow" isn't a disembodied witness standing outside of the experience. Just our talkative way of having it, as much a part of the pleasure as the snuggle itself. Yet it's a way we speak together. Were all terms for my talk with him to be defined by the box itself, or would we retain some old-fashioned ways to converse? Would the computers one day control exclusive rights on our vocabulary for referring to them, with possibilities for reflecting on our experience reduced to glass, remembrance turned to memory, fantasy to reality, micro- and macroworlds eventually indistinguishable in feeling? I moved in over his shoulder and wondered whether he'd just had some "wow" way of being that took notice of alternatives. Did he know he was somewhere special and utterly fantastic, hopeful and terrifying, a world we've never seen before? Was there some irony, amazement, awe, sadness, anything other than facts about missiles to discuss? Could we make talk of the experience and not just the conduct?

After the world blew up, the screen said, "Great Score, Enter Your Initials," and he got to put his at the top of the list. I watched him swirl some knob or another until he made the machine speak an irony, not needing and thankfully not yet obliged to be memoried in the microworld as a uniformly trained PAS. But what he did punch in frightened me:

DOA

"Why DOA, Paul?"

"Because I like that band."

"Band?"

"Yeah, it's a punk rock group."

"What does DOA mean?"

''I don't know, death on arrival, dead on arrival, something like that."

Then what do you say?

INTERFACE

THE PROFESSOR'S HOUSE WAS ONE of those wraparound affairs perched on stilts high in the Berkeley Hills overlooking San Francisco Bay, and as soon as I arrived at the faculty party I spotted the grand piano in an elegant study with oriental rugs, floor-to-ceiling books, as much a look of scholarship as you'd see anywhere. That would make my evening.

In a half hour a gathering had formed around the piano. Then, in the midst of "The Man I Love," there was an explosion in the next room. "Maybe I will meet him someday, maybe... What the hell was that?" my lead singer cracked. "They're playing a video game Herb bought for Christmas," said the hostess with slight irritation. "He couldn't keep it wrapped up. The kids hardly get to it. I don't know if he'll finish the talk he's supposed to give in Frankfurt next month."

Well, we weren't about to give up Gershwin for Atari, about to sit in front of a TV with little plastic joysticks in our hands. So as several people found a polite way to back off and sneak out of the study, a dedicated threesome remained committed to singing. Then someone pretty good must have gotten to the joystick as we got into "I've Got a Crush on You." "All the day and nighttime ... *wham ... varoooooom ... bam ... crash ... bam bam ...* Hear me cry ... *oooooooo ... bam bam bam.*" I played at fitting the "Stars and Stripes Forever" to their action but the timing wouldn't mix. We had to stop. I needed a refill anyway, and the hostess would tell them at least to turn down the volume because they were ruining the party.

The party was in the next room, as many as thirty of them in there at times, never less than ten, and it was three in the morning when I finally left Herb to play by himself. Between drinks and nearly two straight hours one-on-one with him at *Missile Command* once everybody left and we didn't have to give up turns, I could barely see my way down the hill.

Intercontinental ballistic missiles descend from the sky toward six cities on earth, as the player employs a two-handed joystick–push-button device to intercept their trajectories. The stick controls a half-inch-long cursor line, a sight that can be moved and stopped anywhere within the visibly televised skyspace. And with one hand you try to place it beneath an incoming missile, at least if you're taking the game seriously and care about the welfare of Cleveland, New York, or any other city in the world. Atari will take your dollars, francs, or rubles. You then push the button with the other hand to launch an anti-ballistic missile from the "silo" in the center of the landscape to the designated cursor location. And if you've properly judged distance and time, your ABM meets their ICBM head-on and *wham*, the folks below are spared for the while. The overall object of the game, thank goodness, is to avoid the total destruction of all cities. Atari and Company play the bad guys, from any political standpoint you occupy, while you defend whatever counts for life, liberty, and the pursuit of happiness in a world of six towns. Which I suppose some calculate to be enough of a world.

Every so often the onslaught stops and there's a pause that defines a "round" of play. Rounds allow turn-taking competition against the enemy, with no logic except in a truly insane world, but still, a series of volleys is a reasonable enough way to run a war. You can reload ammo, attend the wounded, deal with first strike/second strike problems, or run to the fridge for a beer. Between rounds the score is posted, and a siren then warns of a next incoming volley. The attack resumes. Should, heaven help you, all cities get hit, the world blows up and it's THE END. Unless of course you charmingly succeed in attaining a high enough score to win a replacement city. Points are earned for every successful shot, the destruction of more rapid, accurate "smart missiles" earning the most. These marvelous weapons make a screaming sound all their own, and gain their intelligence in being precisely guided to a city, never falling into the little countryside between towns. Were the cities near each other or far apart, and was their equidistant spacing intended literally or as an abstraction? The scale of things was obscure, and the microworld had a decidedly mathematical look about it. I guess the big one does too when you're thinking of trajectories.

For every 10,000 points a city is rebuilt, though not necessarily in the same spot, and depending on how you imagine the delay between rounds, the urban reconstruction occurs with instant Atari technology or over the course of generations. They don't say what happens to the people, even whether the cities are populated, and presumably considerations of taste have left out burning bodies. Should the score reach the city replacement figure of 10,000 before any town has been annihilated, your silo skills don't go unrewarded. For you now have a "city in memory," which doesn't mean you remember what it was like or even where it was. And when the first one actually does blow up, this remembered achievement makes for an automatic replacement. The memorized city just pops up out of the electric brain, instantaneously appearing some-where else to strategically fill the gap. Early rounds involve slow enemy missiles—carryovers from a prior war?—but with each new round the speed, numerical density, and relative proportion of screeching smart missiles increases, making matters more contemporary and defense more and more tricky no matter how patriotically you behave.

Few temptations can drag me from a well-tuned Steinway on a Saturday night, not into a next room with lots of people anyhow, so the next day I went out and bought a color TV and a home Atari console that plugged into it. Now I'm not big on war, wasn't even allowed a cap gun as a kid, and *Missile Command* models the calculated insanity of the worst imaginable twentieth-century scenario. How powerful and eerie that the computerized arena seduces us to transcend the nightmare it presents.

A whole party full of Berkeley intellectuals blasting their way through an evening of warfare, stoned on button pushing. Sure, everybody made fun of it all. There were the perfectly expectable disclaimers and expressions of horror, enough first rate political satire to give Lenny Bruce a run for his money. Sure, the women came off with the most vociferous disdain. The world was coming to an end. It was a conspiracy to train our kids for the real thing. Not to mention the ultimate destruction of the evening. Most of them hung out in the kitchen, but every so often a new one stuck her nose in the game room, feigning utter disinterest. I thought I spotted some female fists clenched. And beneath all the joking, this guy after that wormed his way close to the controls to say, "Hey, let me try that for a while."

None of us was a warmonger. And neither were our kids. But the pace of things. The speed. The fast twists and turns. The fireworks. The luminescence. Take a Polaroid picture on a street corner in Bombay, a ten-second kind, and inside of three there'll be fifty people hovering around, with a depth of curiosity so heavily smacking of worship you can see the reverence and fear in their faces, whether it's a picture of a dead body or their own child held up for a smiling pose. That doesn't matter. It's the thing in its fully emblematic significance, token of a new world and way of being. Watch them watch your ten-second Polaroid come up, and you can see them looking across the Atlantic. We were looking out there. Way out.

Missiles come in from the top of the screen, the outer limits of one's radar, upper horizon of the new world landscape with its little curve to make your body feel a bit more at home. Several trickle on and then down screen at the same rate, three or four lines very slowly coming from the top. So you've got plenty of time. You learn to move your cursor beneath them, one by one, and without much practice, a half hour at most, you can judge how far below you need to be in relation to their speed when you push the button. And at the time the missile gets to the cursor the enemy has arrived there too.

You go from one missile to the next, aim, hold it, and fire. And that's fine till they start coming faster.

Then you need a new technology for moving. You try machine gunning, pointing all over the place while rapping the button, a give-them-all-you've-got last round of the snowball fight. But the rules don't let you. Only three explosions are allowed on the screen at once, a seemingly absurd restriction in a kind of war where reloading ammo makes little sense. But Atari controls all microworld rules, the umpire is built right in, and the arbitrary restriction constrains and organizes the rest of play. While a three-shot limit is a slight defect in the game's authenticity, along with atonal melodies and replaced cities, its consequences for how you've got to attack are neat enough to make up for it, as with many such restrictions. Machine gunning won't work because you can't keep firing. The video air of memorized places must periodically clear, lightening the electric brain's burden, rearranging its memorized thoughts enough to give new considerations room and time to register and count off paces in the clearing. But it counts fast, thinks that way, and you've got to stay on your thumbs.

One little maneuver I came upon did seem like a move in the right direction. In a simple situation with three missiles coming slowly down together on the same horizontal plane, I smoothly swept right beneath their paths without stopping the cursor, firing *en passant*. When my placement and rhythm were together, as my missiles got to where the cursor had been when I'd pushed the button, theirs were there too. It was a panning action with several little articulations along the way, the hands in synchrony, one wiping past, while the other inserted punctuations. As you watch the cursor move, your look appreciates the sight with thumbs in mind, and the joystick-button box feels like a genuine implement of action. *Bam, bam, bam,* got you three right in your tracks, whatever the hell you are.

When doing well, I could pick off a few missiles with one continuously smooth gesture. Nothing to call the Pentagon about and hardly grounds for trading in the piano. Just a snazzy little skill. But as the game progresses, the sky blazes with missiles racing toward earth, keeping you awfully busy saving the world. So you'd have to have some such smooth way of improvising round the sky, continuously tracing through a sequence of places that wouldn't pile up to overload you, with quick analysis and good handicraft. Just look at the screen in advanced stages of play. All six cities can be annihilated in the first five seconds. The Department of Defense thinks they can handle that on their TVs, and Atari implies you can on yours, so what's wrong with a little advance preparation? Look at the barrage and you know it's got to involve some pretty fancy action. Touch Gershwin? That's another question.

Whether useful or not, my little movement was nice to watch and feel, and whenever Herb took a break I switched the reset control and started over again so I could practice joysticking back and forth, gliding past those slow missiles, connecting up with the lines, each explosion right on the button, each electric roar right where it belonged. I was just as content to watch the world blow up and start all over again whenever things got heavy, playing this little three-note melody to refine the accuracy of my video stroke.

Punctuate a moving picture? I'm no painter and don't dance in mirrors. But here I could watch a mysterious transformation of my movements taking place on the other side of the room, my own participation in the animated interface unfolding in an extraordinary spectacle of lights, colors, and sounds. Improvised painting, organized doodling, with somebody doodling against you to make sure you keep doing it.

The little silly panning shot was a trip. I thought of the arcade and the electro-umbilical hookup I'd seen. I'd stay in an arcade for more of that too, for the flashy lights of the little landscape whose warfulness I could at least pretend not to imagine, for that cursor of pure power you could swing where you wanted, for those wild changing color coordinations and even the little plastic controls that now felt like a way into a new world. If you couldn't take a microworld home with you, I could see standing in an arcade just to be able to put together anything well with the new crystal brain kit, to mount the first step of control over its affairs, its booms and bursts. And especially for action like this shot, with its touch of grace.

Most sedentary, you say, hardly an arena for vigorous action, awfully cold and calculating, the terrain for human involvement reduced from a several acre plot to the microworld of a TV tube and the calibrating motions of two or three digits. The farmer who once gazed and plowed toward an endless horizon now sits on his can in an office scanning a nine-inch video display of his inventory, seedling growth rates, soil composition, market prices, and *Pac-Man*.

But what about finger work in a tightly voiced Bach fugue, or the little movements of writing, reading, and singing? What of Rembrandt's brush strokes? To be good for the embodied spirit certainly action needn't stimulate the pulmonary vascular system. For one thing, there's more time left for jogging when you log in hours at your "PC," and God knows tilling the soil is no great bargain. It all depends on who ends up with the dirty work they won't make robots do. No big software market for street cleaning programs these days.

Human history was cultivated through speech and the motions of fingers, one could say, the tiniest not biggest actions. After all, take away all the carved, painted, and inscribed meanings, the thoughts giving rise to its symbolic significance as a shape, and what's the Great Pyramid alongside Beethoven's Fifth, or something like this:

or this:

$$E = mc^2$$

or even this:

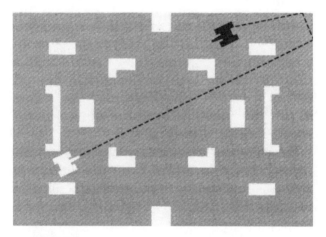

"Just" labor.

Now the computer. Our organically perfect tool. Seated upright on behinds just made for that, our hands dangle near the lap at their most relaxed point of balance, while these fingers, capable of such marvelous interdigitation, have a territory for action whose potentials and richness are electronically enhanced beyond the wildest dream. And the eyes are freed from hand guidance work, free to witness and participate in the spectacle from above.

Before, the piano was the quintessential human instrument. Of all things exterior to the body, in its every detail it most enables our digital capacities to sequence delicate actions. Pushing the hand to its anatomical limit, it forces the development of strength and independence of movement for fourth and fifth fingers, for no other tool or task so deeply needed. This piano invites hands to fully live up to the huge amount of brain matter with which they participate, more there for them than any other body part. At this genetically predestined instrument we thoroughly encircle ourselves within the finest capabilities of the organ.

Then a typewriter, speeding the process whereby speech becomes visible, the extraordinary keyboard for sequencing and articulating perhaps awaiting a still truer sounding board, strings, and tuning, a still more suited canvas for thought.

Then TV.

Then super-fast super-tiny electric switches to rapidly translate keyboard motions into an infinite variety of sights and sounds. Computers.

The three are united. We program the arrangement of circuits to indefinitely vary the effects each stroke and sequence of strokes can generate on screen, building codes and codings of codes, so now this key stands for that, that key for this, dozens of shorthands and shorthands for shorthands. Computer languages. Typewriter strokes get heftier. Sentences gain power.

Then to complement the ensemble further, we add a rapidly expanding assortment of hand tools for tuning, depressing, sequencing, switching, fine tuning, and more. The typewriter is best for linear movement, up and down and side to side, its keys laid out in banks with spaces in between. This word piano can't fill the visible spaces between its printed-sounds, and greater fluidity of motion is wanted for more graphic finger drawing, violin-like brushes to glide and slide over the glass canvas. So there come knobs, joysticks, trackballs, "mice," light pens, and more. The finest nuances and varieties of manual dexterity are interfaced with the televised display. Typewriter keys become infinitely multipurposed, the TV screen leaves behind the human drama it borrowed from our past to get into our homes, and biotechnical handicraft takes a giant step forward.

The full sequencing, calibrating, caressing potentials of human hands now create sights, sounds, and movements. And the eyes are free to watch, wonder, and direct from above, free to witness the spectacle and help the hands along without looking down. A keyboard for painters, a canvas for pianists. With lots of programs to choose from, lots of ways to instantaneously vary and organize the tunings and makeup of the palette. All the customary boundaries get blurred when you're painting paragraphs, performing etchings, sketching movies, and graphing music.

I was hooked.

EYEBALL

THEY WERE ALL OUT OF *MISSILE COMMAND*, damn it. I'd woken up in the morning with the silhouette of that psychedelectric landscape still etched on my retina. Wouldn't it be neat if a "city in memory" came up looking a little different, more imperfect than the original, say, with just the essence suggested? That would at least make it appear computers remember sights as we do, rather than as just series of numerical values for each grid point on the screen. Remembering the looks of things, we forget aspects of them in ways we can't predict in advance, which is to say images live a history within our lives. Computers don't have that kind of memory. How could they?

Herb had another game called *Breakout*, which I'd glimpsed some guests play during time-outs from the favored bouts at nuclear defense. Was there a truly worthy video opponent—a Don Juan of Silicon Valley? Who knew, but the salesman said this *Breakout* thing was a real good game, the TV was sitting in the backseat of the car, and rather than drive around all day looking for missiles, I figured I'd take this one home for starters. How was I to know it would become "my game," that I'd get so obsessed with it as to live out the next three months of my life almost exclusively within this nineteen-inch microworld, heaven help me.

My next door neighbor must have seen me coming in and out, first carrying the TV up the stairs, then the box marked Atari, for no sooner was the configuration set up and ready to go than he appeared. And inside of twenty minutes versus this young San Francisco lawyer I'm in a cold sweat.

At bottom screen there's a paddle, controlled by a steering wheel knob that comes with the unit, along with the joystick you get for other games. You push a button to serve yourself a ball, which descends from just beneath the barricade strip across the screen. Then you hit it back, and every time you do an unmarked half-inch brick segment gets knocked out of the wall. Of course size is relative, the more competent you become the more these lights take on a sort of environmental density and you're pulled by the fingertips onto a full-scale playing field whose dimensions aren't found on rulers.

The immediate object is to chip through to the open space on the other side, and once you've made this *Breakout* the ball rebounds like crazy between the far wall and the band, moving from one side to the other and then back again to knock out bricks from above unless none obstructs its path and it therefore returns down to you. The overall goal, fat chance, is to eliminate the entire barricade until paddle and ball are alone in empty court, victors.

The wall is composed of six differently colored strata, and if and when a ball first gets through to hit the fourth one from the bottom, it takes off fast in a sudden break slam shot and then holds at this new speed till you miss and have to serve again. You get five balls per game, can set the console to play solo or in turns with an opponent, and can of course hit the reset switch at any time to reconstitute the whole barricade and instantly get a fresh five serves.

Within about twenty minutes my neighbor had cut through the wall a few times while I couldn't even get close, and when he insisted he'd only played the game once before for an hour, my evening was decided. Some piano player. As if last night's effort to save the world wasn't bad enough, I must have now gone on for four hours by myself after I finally got him to leave. And by the time I gave up for the night, I'd broken out one lousy time. I relentlessly served that damn speck of light without intermission, couldn't pull myself away from the thing. Two hundred bucks after all.

I tried rationalizing my initial anxiety with the conviction the guy was lying. But then again, he didn't smoke, was ten years younger, who knows? Maybe some basic nervous system capacities were involved, rhythmic acuities different from what you need for jazz, say.

Maybe microworld mastery varied by age, metabolic or alpha wave rates, astrological signs for all I knew. And how about cultural factors? I didn't see a TV before the age of ten, probably haven't logged a thousand hours in thirty years. Maybe he'd grown up with several hours of television a day. For all I knew extensive tube time trained micromuscles for neuroathletic competition and I was thus irrevocably consigned to the video boondocks.

At least the rudiments of slower play were easy enough for me. One of the guys at the party had created a big laugh, throwing himself back and forth while swinging his entire upper torso and arms and almost falling off the chair to hit the *Breakout* ball. He took the ribbing with good humor, exaggerating his incompetence for the sake of the party, but actually seemed unable to effect that transformation of sense needed to engage himself with big looking movements through little feeling ones. He couldn't project a comfortable scale of being into the confining detachment of the interface, couldn't trust the efficiency of a mere knob, but instead handled the encounter like those proverbial preliterate aborigines who respond to a photograph by looking around at its reverse side. The guy acted at the controls as if there were no video fence in the way. It probably took him a long time to get used to automatic transmissions and electric typewriters, not because the skills are so different from a technical standpoint, but because he refused to adopt the postural respect solicited by new embodied equipment. The guy just wasn't a button pusher.

I didn't have his sort of quaint confusion, but automatically made the necessary shift in stance to control the paddle while sitting still in the right terminal position. And it only took a little time to transcend the physical awkwardness of the knob so I could get the racket more or less where I wanted, more or less when I wanted, without too often over or undershooting the ball.

Line up your extended finger with the lower left corner of the TV screen a comfortable six feet away. Now track back and forth several times in line the bottom border and project a movement of that breadth onto an imagined inch and a half diameter spool in your hands. That's how knob and paddle are geared, a natural correspondence of scale between the body's motions, the equipment, and the environs preserved in the interface. There's that world space over there, this one over here, and we traverse the wired gap with motions that make us nonetheless feel in a balanced extending touch with things.

They had it set just right. Held by fingertips and rotated through a third of its revolution, the little paddle steering wheel afforded rapid enough horizontal movement anywhere along the backcourt to handle the pace of action without wrist or forearm aid:

Not like a very fine tuning knob to change hi-fi stations, for with such a gearing you've got to spin the dial to
traverse full field, letting go with your fingers and losing
all accuracy. Very fine tuning knobs are meant for slow
motions, and while you can twirl these dials to reach a
rough vicinity quickly, to hit *Breakout* balls a vicinity isn't
enough. On the other hand, were the gearing too tight,
the slightest motion would send the paddle right across
screen. Ideally geared for travel through the terrains and
tempos of a microworld, the dial had enough resistance
so an accidental touch didn't send the paddle too far,
but not so much that you had to exert yourself to move
through the court.

I served myself a ball. It came down. I went for it and missed. I centered the fingers in relation to the knob's range so I could swing back and forth across the field with hardly any elbow play at all. I rotated some partial practice strokes, trying out each side to test the expanse and timing of the whereabouts, appraising the extent of pressure needed to move various distances at various rates.

I served again. The ball's coming down over there and my paddle's here. How fast to go? A smooth gesture knows from the outset when it'll get where it's headed, as a little pulse is established that lays out the upcoming arrival time, a compressed "ready, set, go" built into the start of the movement. The gesture then feels when to speed up and slow down to attain the target. I swing the bat back and forth to acquire its weight, establish a usable rhythm then held in reserve as I await the ball, preparing for a well-timed movement anywhere within the arc of the swing.

Within fifteen minutes I'm no longer conscious of the knob's gearing and I'm not jerking around too much. So far so good. Slow down, get rid of the neighbor, get a little rhythm going, and in no time at all you've got a workable eye-hand partnership, the calibrating movement quickly passes beneath awareness, and in the slow phase the game is a breeze, doesn't even touch the fingering you need for "the eentsy, weentsy spider went up the water spout…." Here I was lobbing away with a gentle rhythm, soon only now and then missing a shot through what seemed a brief lapse in attention rather than a defect in skill.

Then came the breakaway slam when the ball reaches the fourth layer, and the eye-hand partnership instantly dissolved. *Wooosh*, there it goes right past, coming from nowhere, a streak of light impossible to intercept. They've got to be kidding. Out of the playpen onto the softball field. I missed every one, each time left standing with bat in hand swatting video air. The lawyer had to have been lying, had to have put in more hours than he said.

I tabled my anxiety and simply figured more delicate paddle handling skills were called for. Besides, just as the panning shot made *Missile Command* fun, I began getting off on the action, building control and precision in these gentle little calibrations. With slow shots my gaze could lift a bit off from the finer details of the ball's path to roam the court analytically, to glance at my paddle, then where the ball would hit the barricade, and then ahead to predict where it'd hit the side so I could position myself in advance. And I'd get there, sometimes in sync with the ball and sometimes ahead of it, just waiting. My glance took snapshots of the overall neighborhood, there was enough give in the tempo to allow for some instant geometry during play, enough casualness to the pace that looking could disengage from tracking to analyze the opponent's ways and fit the rhythm of its queries into the timing of the shots. Scrutinizing the neighborhood to learn my way around, I could still bring the paddle where needed on time.

The sounds helped. Every time you hit the ball there's a little bleep, then a differently pitched tone if you hit a side wall, and still another one for each different bandful of bricks. These recurrent bleeps helped you gear into the overall rate of action. The sights helped. The more or less steady passage of the ball painted the action's tempo in broad strokes, so when the eyes loosened their hold on it to take in a wider or different territory, that gently tracing light kept the fingers continuously alive to the whereabouts and pace of things.

At first it felt like my eyes told my fingers where to go. But in time I knew the smooth rotating hand motions were assisting the look in turn, eyes and fingers in a two-way partnership. Walking a rainy street, you identify the dimensions of a puddle in relation to the size and rate of your gait, so the stride itself patterns the style of your looking, how you scan the field's depth of focus and extent of coverage, what you see. So too with sight reading music at the piano for instance, where you never look ahead of what you can grasp and your hands' own sense of their location therefore instructs the gaze where to regard the score. So too again with typing from a text, where if your eyes move in front of where your fingers are, you'll likely make an error, and thus hands and gaze maintain a delicate rhythmic alignment. And so too here, you'd have to sustain a pulse to organize the simultaneous work of visually and tactilely grasping the ball, your hands helping your look help your hands make the shot.

I played around with slow balls, getting the first chance I'd had in years to handle ping-pong–type action, listening to the bleeps and feeling my way round the court. I hit a shot over to the left. Can I place the next one there as well? Of course the lights didn't obey the laws of physics governing solid objects, like billiard balls, say. But Atari had rather decently simulated a sense of solidity. The light came from a certain angle toward the side wall, and then followed out the triangulation by going in the direction you'd predict for a real ball. What about the paddle? Hit on an off-centered portion of a tennis racket or hand, a ball will deflect on a different path and you can thereby place shots. Sure enough they'd programmed the trajectories and different parts of the paddle surface to match, so the light-ball behaved rather like a tangible object, refracting and deflecting so it seemed you could at least somewhat control the ball's direction.

I watched the paddle and ball at the precise point of their contact, refining the control I could exercise over placement. Could I hit it on the left third of the paddle? How about the left fourth? Could I hit balls with the paddle's side rather than its upper surface, maybe useless in actual play but fun, and perhaps good for improving touch? I tried knocking out all the bricks of the lower band before the ball broke through to the next layer, eating corn on the cob. Virtually impossible. I tried putting more English into the shot, coming at the ball from the side and swooshing the paddle across quickly beneath it at the last moment, trying a spin. Did Atari accommodate that? I thought so, but wasn't sure.

It was here I discovered an ethically troublesome defect in the game. I'd hit a brick and the ball would come down. Taking care to line up the paddle, I knocked out an adjacent one, or even knocked out one above it, entering the open slot made by the preceding shot. Again I aimed. The lights faked enough solid physics and the placement was tight. With still more barricade cut from the same narrow region, the ball once again dropped almost straight down as you'd expect. So I hit it square on again to further eat away that vicinity.

Poof. It veered radically to the side, a full sixty degrees off course. I went through the same sequence enough times to make sure it wasn't my mistake. And it wasn't. They'd messed with the rebounds, by God, preventing you from breaking through too fast. A few shots straight up and down to the same vicinity, and then Atari took the mathematically cheap way out. The arbitrary and sharply pitched deflection they used to get out of trouble sent the ball into a low horizontal pattern for several volleys, and I couldn't redress these returns to pursue a vertical attack, had to wade through a long drawn-out exchange until the trajectory gradually became more upright.

Three explosions on screen at *Missile Command* is one thing. That becomes an acceptable rule of play. But an electronic tactic to forestall your progress is another. "All right, veer off to the side. I'll wait it out. Mess with

33

my carefully aimed shot. But if you want forgiveness for being a computer, don't put rocks in the snowballs."

I stored the disturbance like you register a lie on the first date and puzzled for a moment over the game's moral integrity. If the programmer could patch up an organizational weakness with a trivial trick like this, where else might there be monkey business? If it was their way to let you feel competent, giving you three easy placements and then veering off as if you wouldn't notice it, they were stupid. Anybody would see what was up after a few times at the controls. The tactic didn't speak well for *Breakout*. What if she lies all the time?

By this point I was getting pooped and needed to go for the score, to break out at least once before calling it a night. If my neighbor could do it after an hour, certainly I could after three. The slam shot had been putting me out of commission every time. Mostly, by the time I knew it was coming, it was gone. You're going along at a comfortable pace, hit the fourth band, and then *whap*, the ball goes double time on you and you're wiped out.

Now I told myself, "Concentrate." I did a little seat squirm, as when entering a freeway onramp and you have to hit sixty in a real hurry, peeked up to the band to get the jump on when it was coming, stiffened up and sat on the edge of the chair, and handled one. I missed the follow-up but had returned my first slam. Actually, I got myself in its way.

In a half hour of just "concentrating" I'd refined the instruction. I discovered if I told myself to "glue my eye to the ball" I could start fielding first slams much better and get some of the follow-ups as well. For about twenty minutes I sat there mesmerized, tracking the ball like my life depended on it, my entire being invested in the hypnotic pursuit of that pea-sized light. Kneading my eyeballs into the guts of its movement like following a guy in a fast crowd where a momentary diversion would lose him, I soon got to a four- or five-round volley of fast ones. Knocking out that many more bricks a hole opened on the side of the barricade, and I watched the ball break out, ricochet like crazy between the back wall and the band, eat up six or seven more bricks, then fly down right past me. Had I not been taken in by the new quickened sights and sounds, I might have field it back up. My first *Breakout*. Thank God, I could go to bed.

I'd qualified as a contestant, the money wasn't for naught, and I had a good night's struggle. If the slam could be managed and you could breakout in an evening's play, mastery couldn't be that far ahead. Over the course of the next several days, gluing my eye to the ball, I made steady progress. I couldn't eliminate all the bricks, didn't come close, though pretty soon I got to break through the barricade once out of every two or three trials, and after about a week I could get through nearly anytime.

But I couldn't control the shape of things at all, and it began to be clear that there was a good deal more to this simple-looking computer scenario than I'd imagined. It seemed easy enough to get a rough hang of things, to gain a bit of mastery over basic game events. But beyond some rough paddle handling skills I was stumped. During slow phases of the game, at least it felt like some command was to be had over the placement of shots and systematic destruction of the wall. But when things picked up the gaze lost all its freedom and there was no time to see where you were going. On a roller coaster under somebody else's management, taking charge of the action was reduced to your capacity simply to hold on. A discouraging situation. Then one day, as I was just fooling around at some makeshift science, I glimpsed at least the prospect of a more dignified option.

Just for kicks I covered the paddle path all across the bottom of the screen with an inch-thick strip of black tape. I tried playing blind, and could return only very few shots. I shortened the tape to leave a visible slot of two inches on each side of the screen, so when I was in the corners I could see the full paddle plus a bit. I swung back and forth again and again, end to end, trying to assess the gearing sensitively enough to field balls in the wide hidden area. When they came slowly, I could return about sixty percent of them, give or take a little.

Okay, you had to see paddle and ball at or very near the point of contact to handle each and every shot. But eyes and hands could get real close without that. I wondered if peripheral looking could do the job. You may have to see the point of impact, but there are lots of ways to look: out of the corner of your eye, in the imaskemediate background, scanning by, just any old where in the periphery, with the quickest glance. I took off the tape and fixed my gaze right where the barricade touches the edge of the screen on the right, stared intently there without moving my eyes, and served a shot. I returned it. In fact I could play through a long volley gluing my eye away from the ball. Peripheral vision sufficed.

Then came a slam, and my eyes were still experimentally riveted on this edge of the field. How do you like that! I returned it, and the next and the next, handling several fast balls without moving my eyes. Called upon to heighten its powers of observation, my gaze rose to the task. For ten days I'd been convinced you had to fixate tightly to handle fast shots, the time-honored method for dealing with a tricky coordinational problem at a fast tempo. And I'd played that phase of *Breakout* frantically sitting still. With slow balls I tried to find targets, control shots, to aim. With slams I dared not take my eye off the ball long enough to see where I was going, just hung in there waiting to cave in.

My little test for peripheral vision came as a surprise. You could in principle aim the ball right through the fast phase, from front to finish, stay right in there playing all the way, handling fast action and long range vision as well. Looking could stay mobile, thinking expansive, the eyes could plan. The game would take on new character as something more than just an endurance heat.

What was going on? I'd looked around here and there, checking out the barricade, preparing to focus tightly on the contact point for a carefully aimed next shot, readying my look to assist a delicate calibration. Then the slam. By the time my gaze could catch it, and then change over from the speed it ran to get there to the speed the ball was moving, it was all over. So I'd started tracking very precisely in order to be most pointedly with it on the barricade at the instant of rebound. You don't stand still on the platform and lunge onto the train when steps come by. You make a running jump. I'd glued my eye on the ball because that felt like the natural thing to do in anticipation of a slam. So it went, and so I became skilled at handling quick turnarounds. The ball lobs up, then shoots down, my eyes inhabiting it all along the way, absorbing its speed as their own and pulling the fingers to the meeting place.

The experiment made me realize an evolution had been taking place for some time. It wasn't just eye work at all. And even without the experiment I would've soon noticed my eyes regaining their freedom. I'd already been looking away a bit without knowing it.

For instance, after the first few days of intently focusing the ball, I began noticing that my head was inscribing a path that followed its passage as well. So tightly glued to the ball's route, I was now nodding through the TV court as if it were a full-scale handball game seen from above. I look at my index finger held a foot and a half in front of my eyes, my head perfectly still, no sideway movement at all. Quickly tracing the finger a couple of feet back and forth from left to right to left to right, I track with only my eyeballs. First, it's strainful. Second, it feels inaccurate. The finger goes by in a blur at times, is hard to hold on to, and at various places the eyes fall out of phase and move in spurts. Now I move my head to track the finger in the natural way, finely synchronizing the scan. Eyeball movement proportionately lessens, the finger is seen clearly throughout, and even appears to move slower. Eyes don't sense their movements' pace, so to coordinate motions in tight alignment with a visible object's rate, we must follow with other moving parts. As we watch racehorses cross the finish line, our full upper torsos synchronize a pan to follow the heads in sharp focus and feel the winner's nose touch the ribbon.

After a few sessions gluing my gaze on the ball, the eyes were bringing the feet into play. I caught myself tapping tempos along with the bleeps. And several days later still, I found I was hitting fast shots with the slightest little upbeat twist, a zestful flick of the fingers, stylistically accenting this one, then that one, then this one, then that. A slight waist pivot had been joining in too. Day by day the fast breakout rates were more and more systemically acquired. So the test for peripheral vision confirmed what my body was learning all along. Gluing my eyes to the ball had brought the rest of me along, and my look then gained some freedom.

At the instant the pace changes when the ball strikes that band, you at first watch intently for the onset of the slam. But when it shoots down and the eyes try to grab it, they can't possibly hold on not knowing how fast it'll go. That's why we need a "get ready, get set, and then go" should we specially care to coordinate an action at some pace.

As the *Breakout* ball heads toward the critical band, there's no "get ready, get set, and then go." Just a "go." So to grab a firm hold you must possess the game's rates, and supply the "ready, set, go" missing on screen. Your eyes beckon you within range of the pace, but till you more thoroughly learn to feel how fast upcoming slams go in relation to how fast slow shots rise, there's no way at all to ride on the wave.

Playing *Breakout* again and again and again, through the slow phase and fast, from the one to the other to the other, I hit slam after slam after slam after slam, and was nodding, and bobbing, and tapping. I was learning to feel it go fast and go slow, to feel how fast fast is from this slow and that. And just as I may move into a song at the remembered same tempo day after day, I've been going back and then forth and then back and then forth, and it's ready, and get set, and go *wooosh* into this, that, this, that, this, that.

CATHEXIS

LAST BALL OUT OF FIVE. Three bricks left on screen. The farthest I'd ever come. After a minute's break to gather composure, I serve. For some twenty seconds the ball floats off the boards around the empty space of the nearly vacant terrain. A no man's ball. I feel the attempted seduction of the long lobbing interim, a calm before the storm, the action so laid back that I'm consciously elaborating a rhythm to be ready, set, go for a slam. Then! It hits the high brick, shoots down like a whip and I'm right there on time to return. Forget about placement. Just hold on, don't miss, keep the time right, and watch like a hawk for added rhythmic protection. The phone rings. Return, back, return, back. Another one's gone. The caller hangs up and maybe two seconds later I get the last, by God. Can't say who or what else could've mattered at that point. And who knows what I would've done had someone walked between me and the TV during one of the most tense half minutes I've known.

I'd been playing *Breakout* each day, but not all that much, by no means yet your typical video addict. Nobody was around, no competition, just me and Atari on a rainy night. Over the past weeks I regularly stopped in the midst of the action, and suffered no grief for poor showings. I sometimes played sloppily, at other times well, and I couldn't yet explain the inconsistency. About all I could sense was a need for competition, and could especially see a real gain to be had if I could witness *Breakout* played well. What if I'd exaggerated the potential for careful shot placement all the way through? I wanted to see, even hear, the elegance of the game, and lacking a model, it was almost like buying a piano having never heard music.

Maybe I needed an expert. How about a Video Athletes Hotline. "Thanks for calling. Try going for the left side if you're right handed. It's been working wonders." Then the phone incident. Down to three bricks, the closest I'd come, a serve yet to go, the thing rings and I let it. Unbelievable. At my age. To remove one lousy remaining inch-long pastel rectangle from a TV screen, and hear a final inane sine wave bleep.

Atari had me hooked. I've said that before, but this was a whole different business, nothing like I'd known in the silo, or when breaking through, or in handling slams. Like night and day. Thirty seconds of play, for three bricks, and I'm on a whole new plane of being, all synapses wailing as I'm poised there with paddle, ball, a few remaining lights on screen, and a history that made this my first last brick.

Forget about placement, a score, elegance as an end in its own right. Forget about a model of good play to motivate practice. Here's all the motivation you'd ever want: get that action again, those last few bricks left and that eerie lobbing interim as the ball floats about so you never know when it'll hit and you don't dare try placing a shot because you're more than happy just to hold on with your eyes glued to the ball. Please don't miss, come on, do it, get that brick, easy does it, no surprises, now stay cool, don't panic, take it in stride, get it now. Get that closure. Video game action. You know when you've got it like you know your first drunk.

For two weeks I'd watched that barricade eaten away and then reconstituted with a flick of the reset button, the move from everything to nothing never consummated, the gesture left dangling. In the past I'd look at the leftovers, cocky Atari bricks standing invulnerably there. In the first days their looks had no special significance. Not doing anything with them, their appearance was in the horizon of my interest and gaze, with paddle and ball in the foreground. I didn't notice how many got left each time, just the blurred and colorful swatch of a bunch still there. But as I gradually ate my way more and more into the upper reaches, the remaining bricks tempted a more discerning inspection. I'd notice their features, notice the amount of them in general. Not a brick count, just "a whole bunch" left or "a getting sort of close bunch" left or "a hazardously arranged bunch" left. But here, at the end, there were three! Right there, there, and there.

Serve. There's barely anything to interfere with a long end-to-end volley. The ball lofts to the far wall from a slight angle off the paddle and reflects off a side wall back down. Hit it back. It retraces exactly the same trajectory. Fingers tautly poised on the edge of a neurological breakdown, I go through ten or fifteen slowly drawn triangular tracings over the same path without moving. And one of those bricks is right nearby, *oooooooh* missing by a fraction. I'd love to redirect the shot just a touch right now, but that feels unbearably risky and I'm too scared to move. I want that closure, ache for it, know I'd literally hit that reset switch if I missed now. Come on, go all the way, undress that screen after two weeks of dating. I'm figuring at a thousand miles a second that the trajectory is bound to loosen a bit, or maybe there's enough movement in the paddle from nerves alone to slightly change course. Please do one of your dumb programmed deflections right now, damn it, and get us both out of here. I'd gladly forgive you for acting like that kind of a computer. Come on already, deflect off and stop the endless lobbing, do your thing right now while I've got hold of the long rhythm and I'm geared to move double speed if the ball hits a brick that makes it change tempo. For the first time I'm expressly aware of caring about the color of fast bricks. Uh-oh, is orange a fast color? Watch out. Can't let your eyes see just what's what, must be especially careful because the rhythms are so elongated and the fullcourt distance so deceptively slow. Now out in the open, drawn by the eyeballs along an ascending two-dimensional roller coaster, I'm locked on a course over which I dare not exert will. I wait for a hopefully reasonable change in the value of some variable, as I'm moved under strict mathematic control with literally calculated suspense, having one monstrous geometrical high, trigonometric upper, topological chip trip. Is this what they mean by the pleasures of mathematics, when numbers electrically tickle, torment, and torture your nerve endings?

I'd been intellectualizing the game and its skills to engage interest and time. But now here I am with my first authentic video experience, going for the last brick like any kid in an arcade, palms wet, pulse racing, mouth dry, nerve endings interfaced in nanoseconds, the knob itself throbbing, electronic reflections going straight for my spinal cord. I mean way up there with the bottom of the ninth, and it's a long fly ball to left field, it's going, going… Answer the phone before it's gone? Are you kidding? And it was worse and better than that.

Hollywood gets you to cry, TV cop serials flip your blood pressure up and down along with the best that Parke-Davis and Upjohn can offer. A few hours in front of the tube any night of the week and you had to jog the next morning to recover. But now Atari had it, the ultimate adrenaline. Lay out a half dozen lines for just a couple of bucks? A bargain.

Was I hooked? "I've been trying to reach you all day, were you out?" they'll be asking. No way. Not me. Not for that kind of thrill. Not a chance. Maybe at sixteen for a couple of hours. But now? No way. Meanwhile, next morning I was back at it. As soon as I got out of bed I glanced at the darkened TV set and flashed on an image of those last three bricks. Whacky though it is to admit, the very thought of the screen in that state of final tension, just saying the word "breakout" to myself, and I had to fight the temptation to drop everything and make for the paddle, for those last few bricks with one remaining serve, for that supersaturated last lousy square and its intense beckoning desire. I woke up not eight hours later and I wanted a fix, so I plugged myself right in with the first cup of coffee, stuffed to the gills with electric anticipation. Object cathexis, I think it's called. Come on, Atari bricks you. I'm gonna gobble you.

I serve, and break all the way down to about ten bricks on the first ball. Never did that before, and I sure hadn't picked up new skills sleeping. Forget the opponent. When the history is just right, all the intensity you need to motivate practice is right there in the action, one-on-one. Just hook up, plug yourself in till you reach the right dosage. *Breakout* starts taking effect in about two weeks, a hookup per day.

Perhaps they called them video "games" only to avoid troubles with the Food and Drug Administration. Then, too, there'd be problems with the South Americans over coffee, for at fifty cents a cup Atari could take over that market, what with a long-lasting quarter at *Missile Command* worth three double espressos loaded with sugar. How about some straight talk, Atari Pharmaceuticals, tell the whole story. Have you conducted the necessary blood-sugar tests? What about EKG and EEG changes? Pulse rates? "The Surgeon General has ascertained that when used in excess the final stages of *Breakout* are hazardous to your health."

All the while I figured I'd been fashioning a skill. I found a solution for how to handle the fast slams. I practiced. Got to where I could breakout. But now I breakout on my first ball, playing ten times better than the day before, motivated by a scheduled, packaged up, guaranteed-to-thrill Skinnerian payoff from a box they call a "game" for promotional purposes.

I started thinking about these so-called skills. They were odd, even scary. They took place a little too fast for comfort. It was five years at the piano before I looked down and saw my hands appearing to make music all by themselves. But within two weeks at *Breakout,* I watch them handling fast slams, with no consciousness of guiding their movements. And they look elaborate as all get out. Amazing. But what honest basis have I got for taking anything you'd call "credit" for the achievement? I look down at my piano keyboard hands, and a history of struggle lets me appreciate the natural accomplishment they now reveal, the result of a lifelong interaction between a biography and social settings that were frequented, yielding a particular path toward a unique style with its merits and deficiencies. Acquiring such a skill, I have an ongoing conversation with these hands, an elaborate interchange of advice, complaint, and cooperation born of years of collective effort. Here I look down at a knob-holding hand and watch it go through what seem like altogether complex little calibrations. I look at the screen. It so impersonates a real world setting, tennis, say, that I'm taken in by the illusion of adept motion, running all around that court, perfectly skilled at returning shots every which way coming at all angles. I never had such athletic skill before, not to that high a level, and I'd played a fair share of sports in my day. But two weeks? Take credit for that?

The fact is I didn't have to tell myself to keep my eye to the ball. If I kept putting in quarters, or hitting a reset switch, playing the strictly scheduled arrangement of tasks Atari engineered, this calibrating hand would've gotten to the same place pretty much without respect for anything I tried or tried not to do. What "effort" had I made? Strategic problem solving? How to learn this and that? Simply ways to make it interesting. Give the folks a little consciousness so they'll figure there's more to them than just bundles of programmable nerve pathways.

I hadn't forged a skill. Any blackjack player with a night's experience learns the right gesture for a "hit me" flick of the cards on the felt when the dealer's look invites a choice. How much more "skill" was here? Holding your cards a certain way isn't a skill intrinsic to success at blackjack, but a social skill at gambling. And all you need to know on that score here is to keep your body upright and hold on to the knobs at a TV screen, with your clothes on in a public place. If you're too smashed to stand up, they make sit-down models. I couldn't even take credit for "good reflexes," since it looked like nearly anybody who played for not too many hours got to roughly the same level.

A part in an animated movie? Sure, with a script automatically memorized for you. The full caressing potentials of the human hand realized in creative action on screen? Wait a minute. Fooling around with TV graphics and computational manipulations, Atari comes on a surprising discovery. If you engage a human body through eyes and fingers in a precisely scripted interaction with various sorts of computer-generated events, what seem like quite complex skills are rapidly acquired by regular repetition. Sequences of events can be scheduled into readily mastered routines of progressive difficulty, and a program of timed transitions can be organized, programming you, in turn, at an economically desirable rate.

They meant no harm. They were exploring a frontier. We modern humans had become increasingly fascinated with the notion that all things wonderful come from the smallest elements of matter: genes, molecules, proteins, atoms. Now electricity was finally carved down to its littlest bits and pieces and pressed into the service of science, industry, defense, business, government, medicine, exploration, and video games. The folks at Atari had only to use their microscopes to study the chip, that roadmap for bringing electricity into the eyeballs.

How could we not play these "games"? How could we not stand in awe of the computer, the ultimate rational tool, that device that the most influential brands of reason for a hundred years could announce as their perfect piece of auxiliary equipment? How not to be enthralled by the lights, sounds, and colors, knowing they result from the purest modes of human thought—adding, subtracting, subdividing, and the like? No teams of draftsmen laboring frame by frame to create *Bambi,* but simply fingered instructions creating fantastic microcosms, the entire syntax of thinking engraved on a sliver of silicon, our most perfected thought mirroring itself back in a visually moving display. How utterly irresistible, at first, to applaud the marvelous variety of it all: talking clocks, *Missile Command,* word processing, robots, digital displays, spread sheets, pie charts, networks, light pens, missile guidance systems, satellites, airplanes that fly themselves. You can do just everything with computers.

Of course they had a kick at Atari, varieties of kicks. Who in his right brain wouldn't? With a set of instructions you tell the electrons where to go: "Take a left here, go four blocks down there, then make a forty-five-degree turn to the left, take four steps and blow up." With written instructions you tell other electrons to form themselves up into the neighborhood itself, with its shapes, colors, and sounds. You talk with your programmed programming fingers into the TV tube and out comes *Pac-Man*. No paintbrushes, except in the planning stages. Just instructions. Of course they had kicks when movements could be designed, and countermovements made with the fingers, and that interaction coordinated by instructions as well. Particular kicks could be fashioned, as two instructions head for a collision, say. You could play around with the variables and with the body, stimulate little bundles of nerve teasing action and emotion. Thrills. They were thinking up thrills and found that they worked.

There were varieties of kicks, like the *Breakout* kind, an electromathematic version of an ancient dramatic format with its hour-long minute of tantalizing perceptual closure, the pause before punch lines, the javelin floating through air as the Romans held their breath, the dead calm as a motionless deer is lined in the hunter's sight and the body stills itself for perfection. Some kicks felt new, all seemed much heightened by the electric intensity here. Elicited by programmable events, the enhanced kicks stimulated the development of more varied attempts at their own enrichment. Build them up, pack them with maximum density, program them to the tolerable limit for the allocated time and attention span. Now package them into gloriously graphic little fantasy worlds to disguise their real intent and result, throw in some scoring procedures to tide you through the learning plateaus, and call them "games." People like games, after all.

They weren't sure how and why such seemingly complex maneuvers as slam handling were acquired so far. Nor did they know why such neat boundaries could be fashioned to lay out apparently marked shifts in skill at critical yet short lived stages along the way. Add on a slam shot and it'll take several hours to get to handle that. Add on something else, and a week is needed. Build in dramatic moments where the action rises to a certain sort of crescendo. The little skill routines reach a new degree of synchronization, a new stage is attained, and a new excitement seduces further incentive to play.

Maybe it all has to do with the fact that when interfaced on the TV screen, the human body is in an altogether unaccustomed setting, as holistic three-dimensional movements are graphed onto a two-dimensional plane. The *Breakout* hand doesn't move a paddle freely along all facets of bodily space and surroundings. It encircles the knob, to be sure, but all actions transmit back and forth between the mere surface of things. I look down and watch my fingers quickly adjusting the control, the shot made to happen with super rapid, flexible-looking motion. But it's as if the fullness of things, and of myself, has been strangely halved. I could even say that I wasn't so much interfaced on screen as I was "interpictured" there. The potentials for bodily movement and the display lined up point for point as on a graph, eyes and hands in an altogether novel world of action.

Draw a figure on the two-dimensional surface of a blackboard, and you must stretch to reach areas in the far upper corners. The amount of pressure exerted on the chalk further adds the palpable touch of a third dimension. But on the screen a magical intervention destroys all consequences of pressure and perspective. Play *Breakout* with your face two inches to the side and six inches in front of the TV. While the ball is a lot farther away for the eyes, it's the "same distance" away for the hand, with a new burden for movement created along only one dimension.

In the video game, eye-hand coordination occurs in a radically delimited, even surrealistic milieu, all action taking place as though from a third party bird's-eye view. The space of mobility flattened to the non-depth of an electron, eyes and hands needn't attend the forward coming and backward going of things. There is no such motion here. Even should objects be made to grow in size to afford an illusion of three-dimensional movement, that's quite beside the eye's point as regards its task with the hand. Were the *Breakout* paddle mobile along a vertical as well as horizontal axis, like the *Missile Command* cursor, you could move in closer to field a slam shot, say. That would undoubtedly add a significant, if not insurmountable, increment in the skill level needed for the game. On the other hand, if missiles slammed down like *Breakout* balls, and you had to bring a cursor beneath them on time, *Missile Command* would require an altogether different format of events. In either modification, the third dimension would still be missing. You can't move both in and out, side to side, and up and down to field balls, missiles, asteroids, what have you. With movements instantaneously converted onto a flat grid, it's no wonder the little skills are quickly attained. Their size isn't the issue, but the fact that they're embedded in a strictly linear plane.

Isn't it neat how everything fits together? Invent such a game and put it out into the social world. Make it dazzling, no tough task here, so remarkable the achievement in its own right. People wander up, put in quarters, and soon get themselves hooked. A half-dozen lunch hours. A few days after or during school. Two rank amateurs buy tennis rackets to teach themselves the game, and spend the whole summer chasing balls. Two hours in an arcade and you're a gamesman, getting a small dose of bona fide action right off. Perfectly patient opponent, this Atari fellow. It's as though you could be given a violin, seated in the midst of the Juilliard String Quartet, and there'd be a way of playing the music that allowed you to do your part altogether perfectly for a little while before they left you behind.

Put such a game on the market and instantly stratify almost the entire population of the country into dozens of slightly different skill categories. Two players meet, one has a few more hours of game time under his money belt, and you've got a score spread. Any two players and one's the teacher, the other a pupil: "No, don't do that, watch out for that city, you're running out of ammo, remember smart missiles, keep your eye on the ball, there, you're getting it…."

You've got all the resources you'd want for guaranteeing massive social interest: the neurological and cardiovascular kick, and among the most perfect social arrangements for generating interaction. Bless you, Atari et al., you've resocialized us after thirty years of being vaguely with each other during prime time. So what if we're claiming ownership to skills actually accrued quite independent of our conscious selves.

STRATEGY

THERE WAS ONLY ONE PROBLEM. I couldn't clear the entire screen. Not that game, the next, not all morning long or for quite some time to come. Something was going on I hadn't in the least suspected. It had looked like there was no more of a skill to *Breakout* than a skill at getting thirsty, and I'd figured on the basis of that screen clearing I'd been essentially rewired into a competent *Breakout* player. I was wrong. The skills were easy enough to trivialize, but so was my playing level.

Quite without respect for anything I tried or tried not to do, I was brought along to the place where I could come within range of a few remaining bricks with a serve yet to go. But that was it. I'd cleaned the screen the night before as the fresh goal of a first last brick had seduced my care to the maximum. And I'd managed to hold on in a situation that had now become altogether impossible to handle when the synapse leaping thrill of near victory was just a ball's width less intense. The end of the game was a nightmare. And on top of it was the clock, ticking away the seconds, a scoring procedure I'd noticed but ignored, official indication that even if you could wipe the screen clean, you could stand infinite improvement.

I broke through on the first ball of the morning, but finished with a full fifteen chunks left. Still, the new record was all it took to recapture a good adrenaline surge. No sloppy play now, damn it. Reset. The first three balls carried a long way but I blew it again with about seven bricks left. Next round, third of the morning, down to five bricks, one serve remaining, in the money again with the pulse right there in the throat, palms moistening, all juices flowing like the night before. Here I go again, outright fear. I stopped for a moment, took a deep breath and tried to talk my body calm. Be casual, even indifferent, don't scare the guy, make believe you're taking it in stride. I'm racing away.

I served and handled a slow lobbing ball for a while as it worked its way into a trajectory that gently eliminated two bricks within ten seconds. But an instant or maybe two later, my pulse rising a few points per shot, I glanced somewhere to the side at just the wrong time and missed a fast slam. Wiped out. Two bricks left. Just within reach and vibrant with significance a moment before, they now stood there with a put-on video air of total indifference as though I didn't exist. "We'll never again look just like this for you, and you can't touch us because you haven't got the balls."

I stared at those lost bricks, thoughtless, numbed, deceived. Eight thirty in the morning, one cup of coffee orally, three intraretinally, and I'm a nervous wreck crashed from a super-speedy rush just like that. There's quiet all of a sudden, not even a swoosh of air as the shot goes by. That lovely promise of completeness, of that ending, last chord of the symphony, response to your breathless question, the neurological orgasm—Ataris Interruptus. Breaktime, darn it.

I returned to the TV a half hour later, played a dozen or so games and broke through only once or twice, never getting farther than eight or ten bricks. Most of the time there were too many left over even to bother counting. The knob lost its magic. Sights and sounds went stale. And I was back where I'd been for days, a *Breakout* goof-off.

I tried an irritable "Care more." Get that first ball as far as possible and don't miss, just field it, no fancy paddle action, take it through the slam. The annoyance helped. I missed breaking through with the first serve by only a volley or two, then carried the second and third quite a ways each, and canceled out with five or six bricks to go. Then sure enough, just like before, several highwired games in succession brought me real close to the pinnacle. One more time, again and again.

You get within near range of the finish and mess up. The temptation of completion increases, a diffuse subcutaneous malaise gnaws and festers to mobilize a new degree of caring for the first shot of the next attempt, and you play a bit better because each move is charged with an attentiveness reaching forward in anticipation. Shots strung together with want.

Strung together enough for that first morning breakthrough, enough to get down to last handfuls of bricks. But not the whole screen. The endgame was a nightmare. On a good run I got a solid dose of the Atari elixir, the *Breakout* breakdown, the complete object cathexis. But never like the first time, my first last brick. I doubt that I would've glanced away last night.

I tried dividing the action into phases. Just get the first serve this far, the second there, the third here. With two left there'll be plenty of time to spare and maybe you can make it through that minefield of an ending. Don't worry about placing shots. Just have it last like when you first fielded fast slams. If an opening serve didn't get to where I sensed it needed to be, I'd hit the reset switch and start over, without caring to think I might make up for a poor showing on one shot by doing better on the next. And after a while I was starting again even when second serves weren't carried within the bounds I intended for them.

A long fast volley at the finish was simply too much for me to handle. The more it lasts the more afraid you get it won't last longer, and layer upon layer of competing advice rapidly piles up to overheat thoughts to an agitated concentration that melts your cool. The whole field of vision frazzles you with temptation, you stiffen up to fight off distractions, and through that very effort their beckoning power becomes even more salient. Anxiety about the future of the gesture flows backwardly, and you start desperately trying to assess possible hazards without really knowing what a hazard is, all the while telling yourself not to analyze anything. Work over a long run at the piano, a tricky passage beginning on a certain measure in the music. Now play the entire piece, and that fast messy section is coming up. Now you're into it, and in its midst you're feeling a ragged uncertainty in the movements, anticipating just a little too far ahead, getting an image of a bunch of places coming up, trying to have your fingers rehearse a forthcoming movement while you're still executing the one in progress. You struggle to stay in sync with where you are and the press of time tightens, the end comes up to meet you rather than you it, and in the midst of the long fast run you're already wanting it to be over. The gesture takes on a slight gasping quality that increases the chance of a mistake, and when you finally blow it, it seems you knew in advance you were going to, can feel the mistake happening, can feel the slackening gaze just about to do its damage.

Parceling out the addiction and its thrills like junkies are wont to do, I molded the fear and the kick more to my liking. I'd aim for a rough extent of action and if a volley fulfilled that hope, there was a touch of relief and the gesture relaxed. If it went farther, all gravy. Tentative, ragged, and safe in its way, handling a round of play with five planned strokes subdivided the ultimate tension into tolerable components, and little thrills emerged. Fearfully stretching down the ski slope, crisscrossing to safe resting points on the far side, a little spate of real skiing shows up for an instant or two, a small kick in the midst of the terror, and you play with it, try to latch on to it, try to control its details, testing your guts by throwing yourself into the spirit of authentic skiing as you figure it must feel, toying with your fear to risk a slightly steeper incline till prudence gets the best of you and you pull back.

Now having interim landmarks, each stretch forward had a goal, and that began to increase my consistency. But try as I might I still couldn't finish off the screen and couldn't get hold of the trouble. With my tongue hanging out, I was on that plane of being where not even the simplest sorts of analytical reasoning flourish, and with a handful of bricks before me it was pure id, no ego, pure electricity, no program. Oh, please, you Atari bricks.

Day after day I made no progress, the obsession began to slacken, and I analyzed the situation. When I serve a last ball and there's hardly anything in its way, it goes up slowly, hits the top wall, angles off the side, and comes slowly down. You're used to a back and forth rhythm between paddle and barricade, and that helps you gauge how to grasp a slam shot. But when you hit a fast brick here in open territory, you're in trouble. You can't anticipate when it'll come, no way to judge its speed in relation to the pace of the lobbing ball. And it comes from out of nowhere. You might get it from the top, from the bottom, off the side. There's one over in that corner, I think, and then that bunching off to the right. Are there any fast ones in there? Actually, which are the fast bricks? Clever folks, they'd colored third and fourth bands almost identically, while all others were sharply distinct. I'd never noticed that before. It'd be one thing if everything were confined to a certain vicinity, but just keeping your eye on the ball in this holy mess is a near impossibility, near insanity.

If I could break through real fast right from the outset, could keep returning the ball up top, eliminate all slam bricks with the first few serves, and leave myself only slow ones with a ball still to go, that'd be a breeze. Let that ricochet routine do the work for me. It seemed obvious from the start that you tried to break through quickly, but that accomplishment was like an incidental little contest within the larger picture. Now I could see it as a necessity for winning.

Would any kid who'd been around these games long enough have sized up this situation right off the bat? Look at the setup, consider fast slams, think out an overview of pitfalls and traps at the end, and map strategy. No, probably only real decision-making freaks do that. But then again maybe average teenage brains were now problem-solving their way through much of the day, arcades filled with hint heeding, leaving only us older folks, the kind who go out and buy a microworld and muddle our way through the ambiguity of events, even cherish and create that ambiguity, shunning formulas and staying with rough guidelines, maxims, hunches, and a whole lot of improvisation. Only now and then do circumstances arise making it worth a try at enumerating, ordering, tightly scripting sequences of steps toward some particular goal.

Breakout was getting to me that way, I was going nowhere, so I'd formed a plan. The trouble was I couldn't do it. First of all I couldn't seem to get through any faster than I had been all along. Maybe a very slightly higher proportion of my slower shots were pointed in a more consistent direction, but nothing more than that. And I sure couldn't eliminate all the fast bricks on the first four balls. Once and only once, after three days of a couple of hours' play each, I found myself left with only slow bricks awaiting a fifth shot. Something I did made that happen, but not a something I could discover I'd done, could latch on to and repeat. And besides, I blew it anyhow.

One thing for certain, Atari's way of slowing the game in their favor—that sharply angled deflection shot that wiped out your vertical attack—made things a mess, throwing the ball into an uncontrollable wide pattern. How could you quickly break through when you had to wait out the mathematics till you could move upward again? No matter how I tried to cut through straightforwardly, the deflection scattered shots all over the barricade.

Slow bricks and fast ones, widespread distances, clumps here and there. Enough to give you a heart attack. Not to mention those lockups. With nearly nothing on the screen, the ball gets into a triangular pattern so immobile and regular you could take your hand off the knob, walk away for a week, and come back to find it just where it was. Just try tampering with this setup when it's going fast and nearby bricks are leering at you.

When the barricade now and then did open in an especially promising way, a narrow corridor developing in a particular region, I thought I should perhaps try to reconstruct the sequence of shots that led to it. Should I get a video recorder? I was getting nowhere, got confused, wondered whether my strategy was so much nonsense. Maybe you can't win. They just let you clear the screen maybe once in twenty or thirty trials to keep you hooked, and that's all there is to it. You take the action in phases, alternatively try breaking through faster, whatever, and motivation and attention get summoned by merely playing out some such new line of approach. Was I to be a perpetual slave to a minute yet uncontrollable variation in concentration or skill, staying at *Breakout* because of a permanent variability in some response rate or another I'd never surpass? Had Atari discovered a limit beyond which improvement doesn't happen, and I was already there? Couldn't be. That would make the game sadistic. A little torture box, that's what my TV had become. And an expensive one at that. Where's Uncle Milty when we need him?

Then the thought of that clock began driving me nuts. Did Atari just throw it in as a gimmick to create false excitement, or did it signify possibilities for mastery altogether beyond my sense of the game? Once I imagined myself playing the timer, glancing up every few seconds to watch it tick away, like racing an approaching TWA to the airport in a Volkswagen.

I needed information and figured I might as well go directly to the source.

CLUE

I TOOK THE RECOMMENDED FREEWAY exit just past Moffett Naval Air Station, headed for Atari, Inc., and drove through the shadow of two huge gleaming white radar dishes, tilted as though they were really used for something. What about these things makes them usually look like they're no longer in service? Fear, I suppose. And the stillness. Follow Mathilda Avenue, my instructions read, so I circled round that way, these monstrous white retinas still in sight, and now came alongside a massive Lockheed missile installation. I'm looking to my right for the road to Atari, as these strange-looking planes are cruising overhead, one every thirty seconds in a landing approach coming in from the upper right corner of my windshield. No wonder they made *Missile Command* here. Where's that street? Oh, there's Atari. I see the logo. The sort of building I expected, only smaller, brand spanking new, suburban California clean air industrial park architecture, like on every block throughout the Santa Clara Valley, Silicon Valley, forty miles south of San Francisco. Here I was in terrifically sunny Sunnyvale. Chipville, USA. And there was Atari, and those Lockheed experimental something or others overhead. *Bang, bang, bang,* got you three right in your tracks, a nice panning shot out the car window. Was Lockheed a test site for the Atari imagination, or the other way around?

But the guy said Borregas Avenue, so I slowed down and kept rolling. There it was on the right. I made the turn. And there was another Atari logo, and another, and still more, a brand-new complex of over a dozen buildings, large lawns, fresh instant landscaping, discreetly small logos, street numbers, and that crystalline silicon sunlight. Laidback, sophisticated, nouveau riche residences for the Pac-Man family, sleek red and terra-cotta buildings with lots of glass and pitched tile roofs, retinas themselves for all I knew, snazzy industrial homes for *Space Invaders*, *Asteroids*, *Tempest*, and their brothers. I followed my instructions to the *Breakout* place, to the Consumer Electronics Division, where I had an appointment with the programmer. If anybody could tell me how to play the game, he could.

There was a slight confusion in my information. He'd written the program for the home cartridge *Super Breakout,* and that was somewhat different. The programmer who did *Breakout* was now with another company, and I was to later learn that he, in turn, adapted it from a still earlier version. The original video game, *Pong*, developed by the founder of Atari, was part of a so-called "dedicated computer," a piece of equipment with a built-in program to just do that game, like arcade machines. Apparently one version of this *Pong* for home use did include several built-in options, among which was the first *Breakout,* later changed to its present form. How nice to have chosen one of the original video game motifs. Was *Breakout* the Eisenstein of the new genre, Charlie Parker of video jazz, *Well- Tempered Clavier* of the tube? So there were these several versions, several hands involved down the line. Mind you, this all came to fore later. Right now I was happy simply to be near the source of any relevant information, no matter who knew most about what version. My home unit was in the trunk of the car with a hookup all ready to plug into the TV of the motel where I was to hang out for a while since I'd gotten to make the visit. Waiting for my appointment, I was about to ask the secretary if she knew how to play the game well. Tell me, lady, how fast can it be done?

I mention the slightly complex history of the game because a cast of characters appeared in my life over the next few days, each bringing tidings of a different sort. The first chap of course knew *Breakout,* having designed *Super Breakout* with it as a model. I told him where I was with the game, and asked my most pressing question: "What's good play like?" He didn't know of records, doubted the company had any available since *Breakout* in the version I knew was only on home cartridges. But he did know that good players around Atari, those who were

69

into that game a whole lot a year or two ago, could clean the screen on one serve. He wasn't sure what a best score was, had no idea of the fastest times, and was convinced there were kids throughout the land who did far better than anyone in the company. Well, I wasn't worried about the very best score, and the fastest time didn't seem vital. If better players regularly cleaned a screen on one ball, for now that was good enough for me.

Along with a fairly complicated discussion of the game's program, most of which went right by me, he had three things to say that came as revelations. First, in order to play well you had to avoid the deflection shot altogether. Once the ball went into a wide angle it couldn't be readily straightened. Good enough. I was right about that. The deflection occurs on the eighth hit of the ball, he said, which I hadn't noticed that way, and you've got to hit the fast slam band before that happens. Once there's a slam and the fast pace is sustained, the deflection doesn't show up again and you can move straight ahead. No kidding, said I. So that's how you do it. Atari's deflection shot slowed your game only if you'd let it, and while I'd treated it as a form of cheating, the answer was not to have one occur in the first place.

The second piece of news was that the paddle was divided into five discrete portions, each of which angled the ball a certain way. He drew a diagram something like this:

....and explained that the A sections were programmed to produce a low angle, the B sections a steeper one, while the C segment in the center put the slightest little hiccuplike skip in the ball. I'd seen that happen now and then, never specifically associated it with the center of the paddle, never knew what it was about, how it might be used, that it might be used. It was just a little nothing that took place now and then, like a twitch on a chess opponent's face, leaves blowing onto the tennis court. But now I was told that in the endgame, when those lockups occur, you have to hit the ball with the very center of the paddle. This scoots the trajectory over just a touch. Volley after volley you're to shift this lockup over a notch each time, moving the mathematical pattern step by step cross the screen to pick off the remaining bricks. Sure, buddy, lotsa luck. He actually put it in rather more detailed terms, but I wasn't taking notes and missed the particulars. I was grateful just to hear him speak about a "lockup." I was amongst colleagues, fellow microathletees. He even called them "lockups" just like I had. Praised be the powers of a common language.

The third piece of news, whose import weighed heavily on me for some time without me knowing just why, was that there was no randomness in the game. You could theoretically take a perfect path from start to finish. All the angles were calculated, and nothing took place to prevent an optimum game. Nothing except your lifetime. It wasn't a question of taking action in a truly open court of play, but only of moving along strictly determined paths. The angles off the paddle, the angles off the side walls, off the bricks, all there to be calculated step by step were you to bother. Like a piano, whose strings are tuned in accordance with strict mathematical rules, not like a tennis court, say, where action occurs in a relatively indeterminate open space. As for rates of acceleration and deceleration, there weren't any. No solid physics at all. The "speed of the ball" on the slam shot, for instance, was instantaneously attained as soon as the fast brick was hit, or to speak in a more precise but impractical way, as soon as a certain place in the programmed formula was reached by those numbers defining the "ball" and its progress.

Yes, indeed, you go all the way with one serve, hitting the fast slam band before the deflection that would occur on the eighth return of the ball. You then send the ball up on top of the barricade each time it came back down, hitting it up through the same narrow corridor you carved out to cut through in the first place. And you did all that by careful placement of the shots according to the system of angles on the paddle. He was busy that day, extended an invitation for me to return whenever I liked, and I checked into the motel and set up my unit.

How do you like that? Hit the fast slam before the eighth shot, which meant pitching all shots to the same location one after the other. So that's how you did it. Three hours later, with diagrams and tables spread all around the carpet, calculating angles, trying to identify the distinctive segments of the paddle with a precision I could now see was required, hitting the reset switch after nearly every second hit, I gave up for the night. I'd have to talk to him again. I spent the evening serving myself balls and trying to see which portion of the paddle got hit, to see that there were these segments on the paddle, to see which brick got hit for which angle, and then which way the ball came back down. There were simply too many possibilities from one shot to the next to the next. I was miles from coming on a seven-shot sequence to reach the slam band.

The next morning I got up and put in a call to the nearby video game firm where the programmer of *Breakout* was now employed. He was kind enough to agree to a meeting. Like the first fellow, it'd been some time since he'd played the game himself, and he'd forgotten most of the details about how to actually do well. When I explained my last night's trouble in narrowing in on a series of opening moves, he reminded me that of course there was one random element in the game, the direction from which the serve came, an element I'd yet to take into any sort of account at all. When you push the button to serve a ball, there are four possibilities:

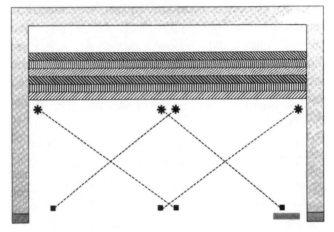

He seemed to remember that only some serves could be taken through the barricade rapidly. He couldn't recall it in detail, but this was a serious problem. He saw these random serves as a defect in the game, for if some were better than others, that made for a significant and uncontrollable advantage or disadvantage on any given serve. Clearly a poor structural feature.

But because he didn't pin things down further, didn't recall which serves were the best to handle, I wasn't any better off. He confirmed what I'd been told before. The barricade gets destroyed from above, you avoid the deflection shot, and yes, you could clear the screen with a single ball. He used to be able to do that himself. As for the subdivided paddle, he asked, "Isn't that in the booklet?" I'd never even read the instructions, but sure enough, under the heading "Playing Tips" it says:

The paddle is divided into five sections. Note that the ball bounces off each section at progressively smaller angles after the third, seventh, and eleventh hit. After the twelfth hit the angle returns to its original size. The ball will speed up after the twelfth consecutive hit OR when it hits any brick in the top three rows. When the ball makes contact with the center section of the paddle, the ball will jump.

None of the programmers had mentioned these angle changes. As for the speed up of the ball after twelve hits, I'd noticed things get a bit faster sometimes without hitting a fast slam brick, but not as fast, and usually by the twelfth shot I'd reached that band anyhow. It seemed to me the Atari instructions were intended for something other than real guides for how to play. Until you reached the point where such information would be meaningful, the details were inaccessible. But once you got to a relevant level of skill, another way of thinking about things seemed required. Maybe some could read it otherwise, those problem-solving types who'd try to figure it all out from the start. But about all the booklet really said to me was there's more of a method here than appears at first glance. It was as if Atari felt they'd better give some sense of its complexity, even a possibly misleading though true description of the details, lest players figure they'd used the game up when they'd reached my level. At the same time, an explicit statement of what good play could bring might be intimidating. The instructions said nothing about the deflection shot.

I continued my search for a player who still remembered just how to do it, put in calls to various Atari offices, but several references led nowhere. Everyone I spoke to had forgotten details of particular opening moves. There were so many newer games since *Breakout* was first on the scene, and while nobody pooh-poohed the game, they'd just gone on to others. Then someone mentioned an engineer who was known to have played so well he could literally cover up the barricade and go all the way only watching the paddle. What more could I want? I traced him down and stopped by his office.

Again, no shot-by-shot guidance. He'd forgotten the details as well. But there were some new insights. The center serves were a mess to handle and he never even played them. He'd serve an opening ball and if it came from the center he'd let it go past. He seemed to remember that no one around Atari played these middle serves. The barricade slot, moreover, was best made on the right or left sides, though he preferred the left and figured that had to do with handedness. As for an optimum strategy or fastest times, he said they never played against the clock. It was cleaning the screen with a single shot that mattered. And he further clarified what the end of a good game looked like. When the game was played in top form, the barricade was always hit only from the top, so as one approached the finish just the thin strip of the lower band ran all the way from one side of the screen to the barricade opening on the other. These last bricks could be then taken off in fairly short order. If you ate into the barricade at an early stage, you increased the likelihood the ball would start returning down through numerous holes, and that made fielding shots more difficult, especially the fast ones. I already knew this intuitively, as one of the ways my endings were treacherous, but hadn't taken that aspect of the trouble to this strategic conclusion. Getting rid of fast slam bricks seemed essential, but avoiding open spaces hadn't specifically occurred to me as a thing to somehow try. We sat around his office for a while as he unsuccessfully tried to recall a specific opening sequence, I thanked him for his time, and went back to the hotel to practice.

I tried returning only serves from the corners, let center ones go unfielded, and quickly found I could now eliminate some possibilities. When a good opening serve was hit with the paddle's center it went the wrong way. Hit on the extreme tip, it struck the side wall and headed toward the middle of the barricade. But hit on the portion in between, corner serves could be consistently sent back to the second brick from the edge, on either.

So I had my opening shot, and now tried to discover a continuing sequence that would cut through straightforwardly. A tricky problem. You had to narrow in on a next shot and a next, only to find that a reasonable-looking opening wouldn't lead in the right direction. A configuration would get set up so that effective continuation was impossible, an angle created for a return shot that you couldn't pitch back, for instance. Each next move was only a candidate, and you had to assemble the sequence without being able to finally decide on any step till all following ones were decided. You had to solve it as a whole.

Nonetheless, after a half hour I came upon a configuration that brought my sixth return to the slam brick in such a way that when it was hit, the ball came down with an angle you could field back up to the right place to continue slicing through. I detected a useable pattern. And then I lost it. What was that? I played again and again, and in about twenty minutes, there, once more, was what looked like most of it at least. And now I noticed not only the opening two shots, but the third as well. So I worked on placing those, and then sure enough, after a few dozen serves I elicited what seemed like my solution again. This time I managed to pin down what the fourth brick had been, and soon all five spots were identified. I couldn't reproduce the entire sequence straightforwardly. But after about an hour of experimentation I was able to visually identify and remember my workable solution. These five shots:

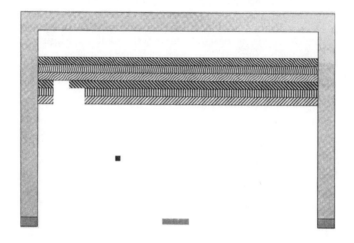

So I began to practice them. A different kind of time at the machine. I had occasionally started over by hitting the reset switch in the past, whenever a first ball wasn't brought as far as I wanted, for example. But now I hit it after every mistake to work on that sequence in particular. Why bother returning all serves, holding on to field shots under that insane pressure just because you didn't grasp the organization of the territory? I'd been playing the computer for several weeks, couldn't clear the screen, wasn't getting anywhere. Coming to Atari to witness a sample of good play, to get a bearing on what to aim for with the game, I was in effect told it's not a game at all. It wasn't that I didn't know that already in some way, but so far there's been nothing I could specifically do with my knowledge that the thing was "programmed." Had there been a public arcade version at which to watch experts' movements, I figured I would've undoubtedly seen good players use their same shots each time. So I wasn't in possession of trade secrets. Just a perspective shift.

The new challenge was posed, the new kick awaiting, the excitement of working out and bringing off a finely controlled gesture that precisely placed each shot. Before, there was just this general obstacle to be somehow penetrated. Now you had a field of completely specific destinations, a sight to be dissembled by taking out a sequence of particular bricks all the way to the end. Surely a more lasting sort of pleasure than the thrill of somehow clearing the screen on the verge of a stroke. With a delicate calibrating movement that attacked the wall just like you intended, you took charge of the equipment. After all, the computer didn't get tired, or lazy, wasn't self-modifying except in ways you could thoroughly learn. All worked out, programed, set up in detail to function in a certain fashion. And that's not an opponent, nor a game, not by any stretch of the imagination. You got a nerve-racking contest only if you didn't understand how to cope. But once your skill brought you where you could see the patterns, or you got some tips you were about to discover on your own anyhow, the game disappeared.

Forget the computer. *Breakout* was a grid, an object with known fixed properties, no more an opponent than my piano or a layout of city streets or a hopscotch pattern on the sidewalk. There's be a game in pitting yourself against another, but "the computer" didn't play against you, not once you'd memorized enough of its ways to know how to correctly use the facilities. Atari provided a challenging piece of machinery, an instrument, a modern moving pencil and paper.

Knowing the general form a solution should take, I took my chances on this opening sequence. It got me to the fast band by the sixth shot, and if that slam return was properly managed I could carry the ball through to the top, slicing a narrow segment from the wall.

It seemed my opening would do just fine to clear the screen with one ball. All I had to do was perfect it.

PRACTICE

FIFTY HOURS, A GOOD FIVE HOURS a day for ten days, in the afternoon, the evening, at three o'clock in the morning, more time on these five shots than I'd so far spent altogether. When I wasn't at the TV, I was practicing the sequence in my imagination, walking down the street, sitting in a cafe twirling a salt shaker, looking up during dinner in a Japanese restaurant at a bamboo and rice paper trellis with *Breakout*-like rectangles on the ceiling.

Every time I tried to hold to the conviction there wasn't any point perfecting something I already knew how to do perfectly well, there was the TV screen, now permanently on, inviting me to prove it. The leftovers of each round just stayed there, going through those endless color variations they'd programmed on the cartridge to keep the tube from going bad, beckoning me like the needle beckons a junkie. The only way not to practice was to leave the house. Otherwise it was like breaking a chocolate habit in Hershey, Pennsylvania, giving up booze on New Year's Eve.

If the minutes of my first screen clearing were among the tensest I'd ever known, this literally nightmarish bout at the machine was undoubtedly the most irritating learning experience of my life. These games sure provoke some heavy-duty feelings. I more than once came close to throwing the knob at the paddle and at times I seriously worried about my mental health.

I inject a warning: Don't take my picture of a *Breakout* opening, or any one of the sort, and use it to approach the game as you'd approach a piece of Bach or Shakespeare, note by note, word by word. Not unless you want to mess up your life for a while. Play *Breakout*. It's fun, it's gentle, you don't have to shoot missiles or people or alien beings, don't have to be a human jackhammer rapping your finger on a button hundreds of times a minute while everything they can squeeze onto "16K" of memory is coming at you. Just back and forth and back and forth. The pace is perfectly pleasant. As the Atari engineer put it, it "plays well." But don't do it like I did, though it won't be at all easy to resist, not even when you've finished this book. And be cautious about "how to" manuals. They may contain the "right" information, with good tips and all that, may give you the inside dope on the program needed to psyche out the order of a video environment. But if they contain news like "*Breakout* is a totally calculated field of action and you must avoid the deflection shot that occurs on the eighth return," they can be guides for a nervous breakdown.

Clearly that's counterintuitive. Surely a detailed guide saves you the trouble of figuring it out yourself, spares you from an unknown opponent called a "computer," conserves lots of arcade quarters. Not true. There's a much worse opponent: a computer program for one of these things that you "understand." The trip to Atari was a mistake, for, believe me, the reset toggle switch hurts more than the buttons in those frenzied action games. After all, if they'd intended for you to practice that way, they'd have made a softer control, put it right on the paddle. They're caring people. Want my advice? You've got to find a way to make believe these devices are games even though you now know there's another way to think of them. Short of that, open the machine and disconnect the reset control.

At one point, a rare rational moment, I tried to keep track of the number of times I hit it, knowing I was in a territory for some altogether novel science. That motivation quickly succumbed to practical insanity, but thinking back now, I'd put the number at something like five or six times a minute. That's about 300 times an hour, or roughly 15,000 attempts to play the five-shot opening, not counting almost as many times I didn't take the serve because it came from the middle. At an arcade it'd come to five grand easy, a thousand bucks a shot, you could say. When I started out, in the first few hours I made the sequence about one time in fifteen. When I finally stopped the nonsense, the success rate was just about the same. Fifteen thousand "one more times" got nowhere.

I should've seen the handwriting on the wall the very first day. In an hour's worth of play after I'd received the final clues I was to get at Atari, I'd identified my workable sequence and made it happen once or twice out of a couple dozen practice serves. Then I left the game, took a brief nap, woke up, went back to the controls, and made the five note melody twice in a row. The first two attempts. I took the ball through my pattern and up to a slam, then broke out and carried that one serve two thirds the way through the bricks on the first trial, knocking out all but a dozen on the second. The best I'd ever played by far. Just like that, "automatically" we say, no thought whatsoever, no problems, the entire little gesture coming off utterly naturally. Exactly like that morning after my first screen clearing, when I broke through on the first serve with the opening ball of the day.

And then it was completely unrecoverable for an hour. That's enough to drive anyone nuts.

What else to do but practice? After all, you need consistency. They told me good players cleared the screen on one ball, and I assumed that meant they could do it regularly. Not just right after naps. I had to find the way to guide myself so I could come to the game, serve a ball, and play well. What else was I supposed to do, make a bad opening and then forget everything I'd learned? What was the point? I knew where that led, to those endings with hazardous holes and crazy mixtures of arrhythmic tempos. I wanted a sample of good play, had received the word. It wasn't until a good ten hours of practice later, with Sunnyvale well behind me, that in the midst of an anguished session I wondered, could pros in their peak of highest form clean the screen every time, one time in ten, once in a while? Even then I didn't mull that over. Get that elegant opening two times in a row where it automatically just comes out, then miss twice in a row when you can't find anything in the least you did differently, and it's awfully hard to sustain a sense of proportion, Consistency means consistency, after all, so I just assumed and kept assuming for another forty inconsistent hours that there's nothing to do but keep practicing. If you can do it, you can do it, period. Besides, it would've been too embarrassing to call Atari three days later for a batting average. Some of these programmer types did seem a bit crazed, but not as much as I started to feel.

I first needed a procedure. I'd witnessed the pattern enough times to remember it visually, so there was no question which shots were involved. And then when I'd seen it happen a few more times I came on a description that nailed things down, a formula that certainly looked like it'd make matters easy. The programmers spoke of this "five segment" paddle, and in those terms my pattern had a fortunate simplicity. It seemed to involve hitting each of the five returns with the same portion, not the end, not the center, but the section in between. I didn't remember clearly what the rough diagram of subdivisions the first guy had drawn looked like, and at times I did think of calling him back for precise specifications. I was vague on just where the boundaries were, never completely certain two successive shots had in fact made contact with the same section. But it looked like that, looked like my five-shot pattern resulted from five hits on this portion between the end and middle. I had my rule: Hit the ball with the same segment each time. That was my first big mistake.

The problem was getting this portion beneath the ball five shots in a row when you're thinking about it that way. But beyond that, this way of thinking about the action begat other ways of thinking, each just as "correct," each just as thoroughly impractical. It takes lots of thought before you learn thought doesn't work, then lots of thought before you learn you can't think about not thinking, and then still more before you learn you can't think about not thinking about not thinking. And double negatives don't cancel out in nonlogical setups, so there's no "final thought" to bail you out of trouble.

I would take a serve and hit the first shot in the right place without any apparent guidance, no thoughts about the paddle, where it was, how it was I subdivided, how the knob felt just now. There were no "be carefuls," or "go gentlys" or "practice playing the old way for a while firsts." My look didn't desperately juggle back and forth between the descending ball and the location of these imagined sectors of the moving paddle, trying to bring my hand to effect a lineup as the two approached contact. I wasn't looking anywhere in particular with a caretaking method. I just watched the TV, served a ball, and hit the first shot in the right place unthinkingly. Then I missed the next. I hit the reset button, waited for another corner serve, and this time missed the first shot as well. Now I did everything I didn't do the first time.

I watched the ball come down. I glanced at the paddle, back at the ball, then the paddle, and then more or less gropingly chose a position at the very last instant and settled for that. And it was wrong. I tried again. Again I tried to see the paddle as a subdivided surface in order to bring what seemed like its second sector under the descending ball. Sometimes I'd get the shot right, sometimes not. It looked like a very tricky eye-hand problem. Even if I had a well-grounded image of these segments, a picture right by my side to consult, moving the paddle toward a descending ball while keeping an unmarked segment of that small area in focus along with everything else you had to watch, that was no small chore.

If only I could get inside the TV and put some lines on the paddle, I thought, change it from a violin to guitar neck with frets to guide looking and fingering.

I realized not even that would help. You still had two moving objects to align at a specific point and there didn't seem to be enough time to glance back and forth to make adjustments as the meeting got closer. One or the other or both objects must be held in peripheral view, or your look has to be somehow fixed in a way that focuses on both but accords no prominence to either. When you're anxious, it's not easy to adhere to such policies. You can try real hard, but there's a limit to how closely even the very firmest of intentions can control looking.

I'd get real close to the TV, figuring that might help, not thinking the closer you got the more eye movement you'd need to glance back and forth from ball to paddle to ball. There comes the serve. Remember now, the second section, just a wee bit more to the left. But look at that. It's not really a paddle, only a bunch of lights going on and off as you scoot cross the graph of the screen. When you look at it closely, you notice what you never saw before, that it never moves continuously, but always in spurts. No matter how minute your movement, it jumps and not glides to the next XY coordinates. Look at the paddle closely, try to very tenderly touch it over the tiniest bit, and you see it for what it is: a set of discrete luminous numbers. Look closely for five sections of this programmer's paddle, the paddle described in the booklet, and what was before a mere extension of your hand lobbing back and forth or swinging away at slam shots turns into a car with two blowouts, bad front end alignment, and a missing cylinder in the fast lane of an interstate highway.

Maybe I can remember the five shots by putting pieces of tape on the TV cabinet to mark each paddle destination, I say to myself, even though it seems that would undercut true learning. It's bad practice to learn the piano by writing the names of the notes on the keys, much better not to use a code, to grasp the layout of things by their own looks and feel. And I can't carry Scotch tape to a *Breakout* tournament. But just for the sake of experimentation, maybe I should try that.

After all, you're so strangely ungrounded here, with no keyboard to get a good home territory fix on, no torso to bend this way and that so you can feel the horizontality of a wall and get that picture straight. I'd catch myself turning my chair into a more en face position vis-à-vis the TV. An obvious delusion. Maybe I could rest one elbow on the set to help feel the angle of my look and deepen a sense for the scale of things. See it from this side and that, see the invisible back side of things through an imaginary bodily tour of the object. Nonsense. If only I could feel the impact of the ball on the paddle, that would certainly help, would give me a tactile marker, stamping the gesture's places into a palpable little signature so I'd feel each destination being achieved and not just witness the consequences of a correct shot. Nonsense.

Non-sense, just your eyes way up top, to be somehow fixed on things in ways you can't feel them fixing, then this silent smooth little plastic knob down there in your lap, and a system of distances out there, neither near nor far away but in an untouchable world without dimensions. And in between all three nodes of the interface there's nothing but a theory of electricity. So fluid, to have to write your signature with precise consistency in size within the strict bounds of a two and three-sevenths of an inch space, say, while the pen somehow never makes contact with the paper. There's nothing much to hold on to, not enough heft in this knob so your hands can feel the extent of very minor movements, no depth to things you can use to anchor a sense of your own solidity. Not like a gun, where the shakiness of your breath and intensity of your heartbeat is translated into a witnessable trembling of arms and shoulder mirrored in the way the target bounces around in the sight. If the control only had those very densely spaced click stops they put on expensive hi-fi knobs, not enough to prohibit continuous movement, but enough to where you feel yourself feeling something, that might get some little bit of the body in the picture. Just non-sense. Just that brainy fleshless electrically engaged being.

As soon as I made all five shots again, I dropped the thought about putting marking tape on the TV set. Every success had a way of wiping out all previous searches for a good method. But then every failure stimulated the hunt for a better one, so when I missed again in another minute, I tried to visualize an imaginary ruler running along the bottom of the TV set to guide my placements. Of course I couldn't really fix such an image with any precision at all, for without an external point of reference how could you possibly hold several spots in view "three inches," and "four and a half inches," and "six and a quarter inches" from a corner? Only for the fifth shot in the sequence was the paddle close enough to the side of the screen, about a half inch away, that I could imagine myself able to remember that distance.

Whenever my opening came out right, I'd try to notice something about how it actually happened that I could translate into an effective maxim. There it is. Oh, I see. I'm not looking at the paddle at all right now. The paddle is in the periphery. Of course, that's it. When the five-shot sequence comes off unthinkingly, that paddle is again just an extension of my finger. I'm not thinking of its parts, but using it as an implement to place a shot in a particular location. It's the aim that's vital. I'm pointing the ball with this paddle toward that next brick as I take the shot, using the projected destination to draw my hand to the proper place. I'm not lining up two objects, just aiming forward. The correct portion of the paddle is where it needs to be not because I've located some segment with my look, but because I've oriented the shot in a certain direction, pointing ahead.

How strange and utterly marvelous it was that in the very first moments with *Breakout* one naturally transcended the artificiality of the implement without ever even noticing it. The paddle is just a straight line after all. The ball comes down and hits this line. Why should the left side of that line angle the shot one way, the right side another, the middle somewhere in between? It makes no physical sense whatever since the line isn't rotating, since it only moves on one axis. As things actually stand, the point on the line hit by the ball should make no difference whatever in the angle it then takes.

From the very outset, however, in your first moments with the game, you superimpose a solidity only the paddle that it doesn't have. You want to send the ball to the left, can't face the paddle itself that way, so the natural rotation that would do that is miraculously transferred onto a movement along a horizontal dimension. You aim to hit the ball with the paddle's left side because you throw your body into an imaginary route as if you were coming upon it from off to the right and pushing it to the left. Yet you're totally unaware of making his hidden adaptation, totally unaware there's something missing.

The whole possibility of *Breakout* and all the other games depends upon this capacity we have to transcend the limited equipment the computer makes available. And when the programmer set up the angles as he did, it was his own body's natural inclination to make this necessary adaptation that provided the background required for such an artificial arrangement to work. Without the natural organic inventiveness of our bodies in this respect, there'd be no video games, and in the final analysis the true marvel of these objects resides in the ways we can instantly adapt ourselves to the altogether meager resources they provide. Were it not for facts such as the natural inclination to push things like balls over by coming at them from the side, and to then superimpose such tendencies onto implements whose physical properties allow nothing of the sort, no instructions in the world could get us to employ these video game controls to fit the needs of the program.

To see the paddle as a segmented surface with preset angles, this spoken-about paddle, undercuts the required imaginary use of the thing as an implement. You can only see such a paddle with a sort of literal look that destroys any sense of "aiming the ball," reducing the task to the matching up of points. That's well and good when you're sitting around talking to a programmer about the game's logic. But when you've got the paddle properly in hand it's a different kind of thing, not really a thing at all, but an extension of your fingers. You bring the so-called "second section" of the paddle beneath the ball in the same way you can move the back of your hand toward a cup in front of you so the knuckle of your index finger touches it. You don't have to look at that knuckle. You're able to direct it to its target because it's just that frontier of your hand as a whole that you're guiding to the goal. Knowledge about the paddle's programmed subdivisions and angles no more truly aids the task at hand than a knowledge of physics could help you line up a certain point on a bat with the ball in order to hit to the field. When a paddle or a bat is incorporated by the body, becoming a continuation of ourselves into and through which we realize an aim in a certain direction, such implements lose all existence as things in the world with the sorts of dimensions you measure on rulers. They become incorporated within a system of bodily spaces that can never be spoken of in the objective terms with which we speak of objects outside of ourselves.

So when I saw a sequence come off well and could see nothing but mistakes to be gained in looking at the paddle itself to effect a lineup, I said, "Watch the target, keep that the central focus of attention, and disregard the notion of a paddle with portions." And I now tried to make sure I'd get a next shot by forcing my look to take in the barricade. Bring special notice toward the next brick, pull the paddle to the right place by pointing toward the goal with your eyes, I said to myself. But that seemed no better than watching the paddle itself, because now instead of trying to jostle back and forth between it and the ball, I was trying to sneak in a look at the barricade to find a target in advance somehow, while watching the ball at the same time. I tried to find a looking rhythm to glance up at the right time without disturbing the shot, but everything got confused. The targets aren't easy to fix on, the bricks aren't marked, and when I glanced up for a specific destination, I was really fooling myself, making believe I aimed. I'd look up, see things, and hit the ball. At times I wasn't even sure whether I just took my look to the brick I was to now aim for, or to the opening created by the last hit. I was trying to project myself toward a target, but without being able to get behind the ball, looking instead at dimensionless things from a perspective that isn't really a perspective at all, it didn't really feel like "aiming." Rather, it felt as though the lineup was being accomplished in another mysterious region of my being outside the realm of command. You don't so much "aim" the ball, it seems, as you must somehow allow yourself to let the aiming take place through a private and inaccessible mode of communication between your eyes and hand.

Nonetheless, in my third hour with this five-shot sequence, I was lying on the floor looking up at the barricade from the bottom. There was nobody around, what the hell, and I was down on the ground right underneath the set, two and a half feet below it, and sure enough, now I could feel a true depth between that ball close by and the barricade beyond. And it did feel a little like I was aiming shots, and I did get several in a row, not that I was convinced it was because I did it like this. But the fifth shot was impossible, with the ball so close to the edge and corner of the screen that I couldn't crouch behind it since the cabinet border was in the way. And back on my feet, noticing what I'd just actually done, I knew it was time for a break from *Breakout*.

Twenty minutes later I was back at the game, or whatever you want to call it, still thinking about where to look, still figuring that one component of what doing something must mean has to involve looking. As if there are components. Maybe it's not a question of identifying a particular brick, I figured, as much as just keeping the barricade salient. Keep glancing up at the whole configuration since you can't really get behind the ball to aim at a particular brick. Keep glancing up so you'll somehow get yourself grounded in the unfolding spectacle and that'll hold you centered. No, that wasn't it, because look there, I just got the sequence again, and now it was really clear where I looked. No question about it this time. I was most focused on the ball during that portion of its flight when it was just about to hit the paddle. That's the spot my look really dug in carefully, in the range of about a half inch above the paddle as the ball came down. Not at the paddle itself, not jumping up and down to the barricade, and certainly not from the floor, but most intently just before the point of contact. That's where you had to look, and you had to look somewhere, couldn't look nowhere. This time I was certain the focus took place right there, just above the paddle. I found a looking method.

But it didn't work. I stared at that place, tried my best, made three shots and then missed the fourth when I felt altogether certain I was in just the right location. Where did I come off figuring I could transcend the unavoidable contamination involved in thinking about the way something comes off unthinkingly? I'm playing naturally. Some first shots just happen correctly. So now I'm searching for the ways of my look as the sequence continues, trying to watch how I'm looking while I'm looking, and trying to keep that investigation from modifying the look itself. Yet it was obvious that the interest the look now took in itself made it behave differently from when it went unnoticed. I asked myself: Where am I looking? Trying to witness the "where" of my look—that motive molded the very look I was trying to analyze. The look searched for a place to install itself to satisfy the question of its whereabouts. Hardly a guarantee this "where" was the "where" I wanted. In fact, it couldn't possibly be.

But what was the alternative? Should I have forgotten about how to look since I couldn't seem to control that, couldn't seem to analyze a correct performance to get uncontaminated guidelines? Then what do I do with my eyes? What do I do period? Left to its own devices, my play seemed to make the sequence happen only once in a blue moon. It was easy and tempting enough to say I already possessed the skills for this gesture, since it came off so perfectly now and then. It must've been "inside me" already, and I'd somehow owned this little route from the first few times I took it. The irritation such a theory created was what kept me stuck in this obsession, recycling through this opening sequence like crazy while at the same time having to continually ask myself why in the world I was working on something I already knew how to do. Perhaps it wasn't so much "learning" I sought, as much as sort of proof of ownership. I'd really have it when I could do it again and again and again.

I had to make that happen. If I couldn't inspect the ways I behaved when it went well in order to discover a useful maxim, was I at the mercy of some unknown inner whim, reduced to sitting back and waiting for a lucky moment? Of course I could've supposed that if I didn't try to get it right, but just kept playing some way or another, it'd display itself more regularly. But then again there it came, done just right, staring me right in the face with all the feelings about what it was like when it just happened this way, tempting me, asking me to thoughtfully retrieve them.

Some science was called for. I put a small piece of tape right smack in the middle of the TV set and stared there, fixing my gaze. Well, I'll be darned. I could make shots without following the action; keeping both paddle and ball in peripheral sight it was still possible to effect a lineup. Just like earlier, when I discovered I could handle fast slams without focusing on the ball itself. This seemingly most delicate alignment between a descending pea-sized ball and an eighth of an inch portion of a moving paddle could be achieved without a directed look. This obviously most acutely demanding task for eye-hand coordination could be accomplished in the periphery. Amazing, the powers of the eye. Amazing how we pay attention to engross our being in events, only to discover a focused look wasn't a necessary component of the task but only the means whereby we brought ourselves before it. Amazing how when in trouble we watch more precisely, when that's seldom the actual organic root of the problem or its solution.

But before, the discovery that slam shots could be fielded without gluing onto the ball signified the emergence of a freedom. There was the prospect that my eyes were able to attend various features of the unfolding display in order to place shots without being locked up in intense ball tracking, holding on to a roller coaster with no room for creativity. The question now emerged as to what there was for my eyes to do at all. Out of the corner of my gaze I can achieve the desired result, so the effort to finely hone my look was off base. Watching closely felt naturally needed. That's what we do when we've got to perform in a minute setting of sights and actions. But usually, when the intensity of such attentiveness falls off and the work gets accomplished through a more casual sort of regard, the gaze is then employable in the interests of other goals. Here, however, there was nothing to be gained in roaming about the spectacle as a whole, since all the shots were already decided in advance. So what active work did looking have left for itself? With it now apparently unnecessary for ball and paddle to be in the foreground of my gaze, and with the sequence decided in advance so no visual creativity was called for over the course of play, the look had no particular need to be put anywhere in particular at all. Everything could be on the horizon. It was as though I had to look not to thereby actively achieve anything, but only so the necessary inner circuitry could run through me. My gaze could function in the most minimally mute way as merely the vehicle by which I was wired into the setup. The fixed stare sufficed.

I can play the piano with my eyes closed, and should I gaze out at a crowd, seeing nothing in particular since the music fills my body, that's an acceptable condition for being when sounds are what counts. But here I'm presumably into a visual enterprise, and yet there's nothing in particular I need look at. How utterly strange and utterly scary. Something very odd was at work.

I'd been trying this thing now for some hours, twenty minutes here, forty-five there, maybe a full hour spent trying to analyze and control my look. Still, the same degree of consistency. I get it twice, sometimes three times in a row, then a half-dozen trials with most shots right, then a bunch where the whole sequence is entirely out of hand. By working on this opening sequence maybe I'd forgotten the feeling of the game as a whole, I reasoned. That engineer fellow just played away like any novice while we talked, reacquainting himself with the spirit of the game, hitting all balls, warming up. That's it. I need a warm-up. My hand is probably a little stiff. Give me some good old slam shots where you swing back and forth across the full territory. It'll loosen me up. Get on the basketball court and you take shots from all directions, layups, jump shots, hooks. Limber up. Too bad its pace isn't controllable. I'll rehearse for a while.

Forget everything you know and just play like you used to. How much of a warm-up makes sense? I'm impatient to see if it works. A minute of old-fashioned play. Fine. Let's see if that helped. Back to the sequence. I got the first four shots, missed the fifth, hit the reset button, tried again, same results. First four right, fifth wrong. Hit it again, and that was the end of the warm-up. But how much had to do with the flexibility of my hand anyhow? Try it with the left hand. I can't delicately manage any small movements with my left hand except at the piano, but sure enough I got three shots correctly, right off. The only problem was a peculiar confusion about direction, and if I reminded myself which way I had to move, I could overcome that, and my accuracy seemed as high as with the right hand. How striking. Try to write your signature with your wrong hand and it's a nightmare, so it appeared this calibration actually involved very little of what we'd call manual dexterity and coordination, potentials thought to reside somewhere in the musculature and tonal sensitivity of the organ itself. I stuck the control in my mouth, not turning the knob but its receptacle, and even this way I could hit shots. Put it on the floor and use my big toes to swing the paddle. Again I hit two shots right. Unbelievable. The distance on the knob to move from any one shot to the next is probably on the order of a quarter of an inch at most, and I could do it with my toes.

So rule out the notion accuracy depends on the physical readiness or flexibility of any particular body part. But that left me nothing I could use. I couldn't find where to keep my eyes, couldn't see any sense getting the juices flowing to a specific organ. Crack my knuckles, shake my hand to loosen up the wrist? Why bother if I could do it with my toes, my mouth, the left hand. I couldn't find a locus for the skill. Mastery seemed to lie somewhere deep inside, instead of on the sort of a surface I know how to intentionally employ.

This time I'm going to get the thing. Be real careful. I serve. I get the first shot right. There's the return, and it'll come right about here, and I'm right about there. Don't miss. Got it. It goes up, hits the correct brick, here comes the return, it's going to be a little farther to the right now, so I'm moving to the right. Be careful, don't go too far. So I don't go too far because I'm scared, and instead of bringing the second section under the paddle I bring the middle under it and the ball shoots off to the far right side. Be more careful. So exactly the same thing happens three times in a row, the third shot always hit fearfully in the middle with a full paddle that can't miss the ball but can't hit that brick.

I'll pretend it doesn't matter, since I can immediately witness the consequences of caution. Be casual this time and make believe you couldn't really care less one way or the other. Get back that naturalness you had when you woke up. So I go again, and the first two shots are fine, and now comes that third one a little farther to the right, and I'm so casually pretending it doesn't matter that I swing broadly and nonchalantly in that direction, while before the movement to this side was cautious. And now I hit the ball on the very tip of the paddle, which sends it to the left wall. Be real careful and act scared, and you don't move far enough so the ball goes to the right. Tell yourself to be cool about it and you overdo the movement and almost pass the ball, tipping it too far to the left. Watch the angles of your emotions precisely rendered as the mathematics display vectors of your moods.

Back again, I'm into the same sort of bind, only this time it's the fourth shot That's troublesome. Too much caution with that fourth shot, twice in a row, so I'll relax more, and once again my "relaxation" shows up in a mistake from the other direction, the same pattern as before. It's somewhere in the middle; somewhere between caution and feigned indifference lies the correct emotion and the correct angle. Confident assertion, perhaps. Caution is forty-five degrees to the left, studied nonchalance forty-five to the right. Maybe confident assertiveness bisects those two emotional stances. The psychologists have been trying for years to put moods on a linear scale. *Breakout* goes them one better. Take the angles right off the screen, no need for interpretation, the ultimate projective test. Self-administered and -scored, you've got the computer program to analyze your results contained right within the program of the game itself. Get rid of all that fuzzy talk about moods, and finally bring feelings down to the mathematical place they belong, so psychology departments in the university can cash in on all the new dough that's available. And therapists in California always looking for a new gimmick can talk about "neurolinguistic programming" and have some hard science to back them up. Watch your moods realized in the pure mathematics of an algorithm, start dreaming about *Breakout* angles instead of your mother, and it's bye-bye Freudian, hello Nerdian psychology.

Confident assertiveness, that's what I need to dissect the angle in half, but of course now the shot goes somewhere altogether else. Hit the reset switch again, and this time as I come upon the fourth shot it has now become just that place where I'm having some sort of trouble in general. The history of caution followed by nonchalance quickly fades into the past and this fourth place is now a fragile overall region within the gesture where I don't know which way to go. Errors start to ripple backward as I'm coming up on this diffusely troublesome fourth shot, and now the third one goes haywire, on the cautious side of course, the fear creeping up. Reset. Serve. One, two, then again three misses on the cautious side. Three times in a row the third shot is too uptight, so the whole internal dialectic of moods gets set up again one step back up the line. Soon I miss the very first shot as the entire effort turns into a dulling mess.

But now I've got something to go on, seeing the patterning of errors in this fashion. It's my "attitude" that matters, whether I'm anxious or cautious, overzealous or too cool. It's not a mechanical problem, what to look at to effect a lineup, how to aim shots. It's all a question of one's overall state of involvement, of the most minute ways fear, impatience, anticipation, boredom, determination, and the rest creep into mess up the gesture. So slow things down, I say, still the mind by immersing being in the unfolding moment, dig into the ball, and let its pace become the sole theme of your scattered consciousness. Slow down and let the gesture unfold from place to place, let its continuous sway even out the rough edges of your momentary moods.

I'm rising up with the shot then, the volume turned up high now, filling the room with bleeps, and I'm putting the shoulders and head into the action, singing a song with this ten-second sequence. I'll make up for the lack of heft in this knob by enveloping the frictionless calibrations in an encompassing style of undulating. Hum the sixteen-note melody created by the bleeps when the ball hits paddle, bricks, and side wall. *Bleep*, the serve... *bloop*, the return... *blapbleep*... a quick brick bounce off the side wall back down to... *bloop*, the next return after the beat, and then up, down, off the side back up, *bleep* back down, up down, off the side down up. Throw yourself into the unfolding melody, carry the hand smoothly from one point to the next, ride with the ball through the whole five places. With that kind of a melody? How? It's not like this:

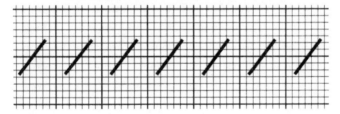

but this:

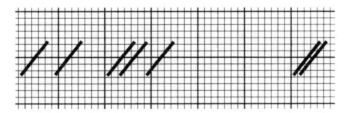

And I can't sing that. It has no rhythm, has no unfolding, it's not a smooth movement, only smoothly like the glassy TV screen. I've got the rhythm. It's got nothing but a formulaic pulse, so irregular it's impossible to sing. Even in one of those Bartok pieces where the meter changes every measure, you've got an accent, you've got the movements of a timekeeping body. Here you've got a string of sighted sounding by-products of electrical timing routines. No accents, no force, no regular intervals between any events in the five-shot opening, the ball floats down along its own checklist in a nongravitational field, the elapsed time from any one point of articulation to the next purely a function of the varying distances between them.

I rise with the first shot, no problem, pushing my head up toward the peak of its ascent, and the ball hits the brick. No it doesn't. I wish it struck the barricade, wish it surged forward and surged back, so as I surge along pushing and recoiling there wouldn't be those blank spaces while I wait for the ball to catch up or fall behind. It has a rhythm filled with empty time, while mine is compacted, full and dense. The gesture of the five-shot opening doesn't flow from one spot into and through the next. Between any hit and those following, from the standpoint of my body there are altogether unrelated changes in rhythm. I hit the serve, *bleep*, the ball comes down. I hit a return, *bloop*. I've got a "ready," and then a "set," and my head rises toward a "go." But the ball hits the brick just the slightest bit later than the beat, and because there's no thrust in this world, I have no way of assessing when the shot will reach its target. If I hit an actual ball, the force of my movement arises out of a preparatory rhythmic surge that goes forward toward that time when the ball reaches its destination. My body has the mysterious ability to instantaneously take into account the force of my movement and the perceived distance and direction to be traveled, and to place these variables into a simultaneous equation that allows me to literally touch the time and place of arrival.

Here, however, as soon as the ball contacts the paddle, my intervention is thoroughly neutralized. I reach with an established pulse toward the next node of the melody. The ball comes down and I'm moving to bring the paddle to the right location in time with that pulse. But the ball won't be at the paddle when any next body beat would occur. So as it comes down toward its next point of contact, I'm thoroughly dependent upon the eye's guidance to remind me of the steadiness of the ball's movement and to neutralize any surge toward a next pulse that would in fact produce a mistake. As the ball traces through the sequence at a perfectly constant speed, any attempt to make a melody of this course of movements, to grasp it as a human gesture, comes up against an insistent mathematical irregularity where melodies can't exist. From each shot to the next I must latch on to the ball anew to give my hand a next time of arrival completely independent of what happened before, so the attempt to establish an unfolding rhythm to link up one shot to the next is forever undermined and altogether pointless. Slow it down and get your body into a rhythm, and that can make you feel like you're beginning to mold the shape of events. But it's all just cut loose from you. *Bleep … … bloop … beep … … … bleep … … bloop … bleep … … bloop … bleep … beep.*

Dealing with fast slam shots in relation to the slower lobs, it felt like I'd acquired an overall rate shift to make the transition. But the action at that stage was so gross. While my own body's pulsing sufficed to aid the tempo shift there, creating an illusion that the shots surged forward with a true rhythm, here the lack of any thrust in the ball made itself known, frustrating any effort to coordinate movement in the customary ways.

Where can I put my eyes? How can I organize a way of moving that will pin down these five shots? The moods that arise in the course of this frustrating struggle produce all sorts of minute hesitations, flutterings, and twitchings, and I can't hold the movements under control by tightening up the time, can't link each shot to the next by translating some effective emotional stance into a way of consistently pacing my play. Somehow the eyes and hands must be freed to participate in a secret alignment I disturb whenever I try to intervene.

What's more, persistent errors of a systematic nature occur at a level over and beyond what I can detect as the result of some obvious emotional disturbance. Errors arise from neurological factors, perhaps, from sources inaccessible to introspection and probably resistant to my will even were I to identify a way to employ it. There's the undershot of caution, the overshot of nonchalance, and generalized disturbances created by indifference, tiredness, a lack of motivation. These I can at least recognize and strive to correct, however unsuccessful I might be. But what to do about strange inexplicable little kinks that now and then arise in the gesture, persistent errors whose origins I can't commonsensically trace? I get up from a rest and four times in a row I miss the first shot in the same way. I leave the game for a full day and find that an unfamiliar three-shot arrangement that occurred at the beginning of some prior session is now back again. I spend an unproductive half hour fooling around to see if I can place a first shot to a new location, to the brick at the very edge of the barricade instead of the next one over, for example. It seems impossible. But the next time at the controls I hit this new brick three times in succession. What do I do about mistakes that look like those strange typing errors that get set up and become altogether resistant to remedial action. I mistakenly type "perhaps" as "perhpas," and then for weeks the defect recurs. I attempt to excise the error with the typically successful technique of slowing down the movements, taking it up a letter at a time and firmly reimplanting the right sequence in a self-conscious way. Yet back it comes again two days later, perhpas, or perhsap, stubbornly ingrained in some thoroughly mysterious and inaccessible way. Enough to make you believe in "brain tracings" and similar mythologies. So too here, such troubles now and then occur without any seeming provocation or direct relation to a recognizable defect in attention, will, or motivation.

It's as if some motionless, thoughtless, lookless action is needed to get things to happen right, that I must suppress all grace and care and conform my own attitude into the sort of a being through which the calculations can pass. It's as if instead of truly incorporating the events on the screen within the framework of the body's natural way of moving and caring, the action on the screen must incorporate me, reducing or elevating me to some ideal plane of synaptic being through which the programmed coincidences will take place. Of course in principle I don't mind being turned into a chip. It all depends on what it feels like to have the calculated currents run through me and organize my conduct. Once I find the proper approach and get through this impasse, should I live so long, perhpas [sic] I'll discover a Silicon Zen far surpassing anything meditational consciousness has yet come up with?

Midway through my fifty-hour siege, still trying to pin down necessary ingredients for consistency, still trying to find a place for consciousness to install itself in these affairs, my thoughts and conduct had spiraled into typical philosophic nonsense. Do I really "know" the sequence, have I learned it, or am I simply in pursuit of a set of events I can intellectually recognize as the ones I seek? Has the sequence been acquired as some sort of an imprint, or is every trial just another go at an "it" that's actually discovered anew on each occasion, shot by shot. That would make practicing totally senseless. I'm trying to perfect a sequence of movements, or so I figure whenever I don't stop to seriously wonder why it just comes out so perfectly now and then. To practice implicitly assumes that sooner or later the effort will add up to some lasting attainment, and the whole struggle rests on the conviction that consistency will arise when the gesture is finally pinned down in a permanent way.

To test what I knew, I hit a shot and closed my eyes just before it reached the intended target. Did I know which way to go for the next shot without having to watch to see the direction? Yes. I hit a serve, closed my eyes, and moved the paddle to the appropriate side. But if all I knew was the right direction, that could be the consequence of a thought, I thought: "go right now," "shot number four is to the left," and so on. How accurate was my blind movement? That was the important question. Several more trials and I found I could on occasion bring the paddle to just the correct spot for a next shot without looking once I'd hit the one before. Now that certainly seemed like body and not mind knowledge, I reasoned, surely seemed as if my hand and who knows what other parts of me had acquired the particular shape of these movements. A relief. At least there was nothing in principle that made practicing the moves an absurd thing to do. At least there was a "something" that'd been acquired here. Not that that discovery had any practical bearing whatsoever.

In fact, my natural assumption of an objective existence of the five-shot ideal underlied all sorts of utterly ridiculous habits. I made a mistake on the second shot, so now that had to be corrected. "The gesture" was in trouble there, I quite naturally thought, not "now I'm doing this, and before I did something different." And when an error occurred on the next trial with the same shot, how could I not see it as a "repeating same error"? Chronic troubles in particular regions of the gesture, persisted for a while and had to be cleaned up. A half hour later the fourth shot was consistently off, while the second was doing just fine, so I had to repair it. Then the third one faltered. Fix it up. Now the second was off again. I treated each error as the sign of some local weakness in the sequence, the sign of a raggedness in the movements rather than trouble at another level. Still thinking, still practicing note by note, still insisting it was an already established gesture to be somehow acquired with a yet firmer command. Not knowing what else to do, I stubbornly dwelt within this opening pattern, patching it up here, then there, then back here again, cycling over and over in a persistent and increasingly nutty attempt to fix something that needed fixing all over, never stayed fixed, and then now and then happened as though it'd never been broken in the first place. It wasn't yet firmly known, I still couldn't help but think, no matter how unselfconsciously it'd now and then simply happen. Every time the pattern came off, all I could see was the occasion to try a repetition so I could count on finally having the thing at my disposal.

I did it right, carried the ball through the barricade and played it down quite a way till I missed a shot. I hit the reset button and made the sequence again. That's twice in a row. Then right after successfully hitting the fifth brick, without volleying the ball further, I hit the lever once more to see if I could go for three times. Practice makes perfect, and on each repetition the very feeling of doing it still again makes up the growing sense of security. I was finally acquiring it, I thought. One more time. Made it again. Hit the button after the fifth shot and go for still more proof. I messed up the fourth trial. Three successes. Still not perfection. Still not enough to be sure that on any occasion I'd come to the game, serve a shot, and go the whole way. Not yet enough to finally put the opening to rest and go on from there. I practiced and practiced without realizing that the very thought of a "five-shot sequence I want to see if I can get again" was bringing just that sort of attention to the action that guaranteed the very troubles I tried to avoid. As I persisted in the unspoken belief that some parts of me had yet to learn this maneuver well, even though I couldn't find anything to do concretely to enable improvement, the thought of a trial hovered over each step along the way. And that undermined success, undermined my life as I walked through the streets seeing rectangles.

I also did foolish things like this. One day I discovered another sequence, another five- or six-shot opening that worked as well as the first. The new sequence involved a slightly different way of playing the third and fourth shots, but it brought you up to a slam brick before the deflection, cutting through the barricade almost the same way as my original solution. This alternative happened several times in one hour that day, and I went through a little trauma trying to decide whether to nail it down.

First, since it came out several times in a row, I had the ridiculously absurd thought that perhaps it would be easier to master than the other one. Then of course I lost it. The question was whether I should try to reconstruct it in the same terms I'd constructed my original solution. In order to make it available for use, I figured, I'd have to recover it specifically, to enumerate the order of the bricks and then identify the paddle sections and angles that produced it. That's how I knew my first sequence, so that's how I'd need to learn this one. And the first few times I saw it, and saw that it worked, I was a bit uncertain about just what the order of shots had been.

But then if I identified and continued to practice this alternative, I'd forget my original one, I thought. I suppose I'm capable of handling a bunch of opening sequences. Certainly it couldn't hurt to have two. It's not a question of what I can hold in my head, because I can certainly remember many patterns and their looks. But until I securely possessed my original solution, I didn't want to take any chances practicing another. I might further forget the feeling of the first one and it was still altogether too slippery and elusive. If I learned a new third shot, say, and did that several times, it might replace the old third one. The new arrangement would get embedded in my body and there'd be confusion between the two sequences. I have no trouble playing thousands of melodies at the piano, but that's because I've gained a generalized capacity to handle whatever comes up as they unfold, and I can play any ones I want correctly and consistently all night long. Still thinking of a skill, somewhere inside me, I couldn't chance contaminating my primary movement with the intrusion of another gestural form. So I avoided the use of this alternative opening sequence, specifically inhibited myself from remembering its organization, staying with the movements that were still "in trouble."

COIN

AFTER ONE LAST PSYCHOTIC EPISODE at the controls I nearly came to my senses. I stared at the TV for six nonstop hours, hitting the reset switch again and again like a homebound Vegas gambler feeding slots at the airport beyond all hope of success. Every time bunch of strawberries lands in the right-hand column and he gets back two coins for one, he's more nervous they'll call his flight before the final quarter is spent. Forget a last-minute jackpot. Lose, damn it, at just the right pace to fill the remaining moments in town with action, with just the right final dab of remorse to round out the vacation. Take all my money but let me keep pulling the handle until it's time to go.

I did have a plane to catch, for I was off to New York. I'd hang out at museums, wanted to look at those Dutch realistic paintings from the seventeenth century where the light of a dimmest room suffices to reflect a blazing midday sun that illuminates an entire world, where you can't control brightness, contrast, and tint from behind, where the brilliance magically resides on the texture of the three-dimensional canvas itself. Nice artifacts against which to place these luminous microworlds in historical, technical, and aesthetic perspective. I'd hang out at the Met and the Modern, take in Broadway and some new movies, juxtapose other entertainments alongside those found on the boulevards of Silicon Valley. And the green you saw there was mostly televised on computer consoles, while it was springtime in Central Park.

It'd been years since I frequented Bradley's in the Village, and Ron Carter was scheduled there. So I'd catch the finest jazz bass that ever happened, watch him embrace that luscious hunk of hand hewn wood to fill the room with melodies a lot heftier than *bleep … bloop … bleep … bloop … bleep … bleep.* They were even on the airplane, those bleeps. Two guys in the seat in front of me were beating up a wristwatch in some game to keep the numbers from moving across the display, while on the other side of the aisle a woman was reminded of the precise time every fifteen minutes as if she were personally responsible for checking our remaining fuel supply.

It'd reached the point where I was as much immersed in doing it wrong as doing it right, and when I plugged into the TV at the American Stanhope Hotel across the street from the Metropolitan Museum of Art at four o'clock on a beautifully sunny afternoon, fifty steps from the Park, and spent my first hour and a half in town trying to eradicate a strange new mistake with the third shot exactly the same as I'd made on the very last few trials with my sequence before packing it up in Berkeley—well, that did it. The obsession finally revealed itself in its richest insanity. Thank God there were no Japanese restaurants in the neighborhood.

I knew my approach had been basically absurd, but I couldn't stop myself, couldn't drop the melody analogy, couldn't get rid of the absurd orientation to skill and consistency. I knew I was going about things backward, but to stop trying to master what so much felt like a thing you should work on, ran too much against the grain of everything I knew about how to learn something with one's hands. That reset button was an engineering mistake of the first magnitude when used as I'd used it, embodying the most ontologically and metaphysically curious notions, a token for perhaps the biggest mind-body conflict to hit the scene since Descartes first got us into serious trouble.

Walking down Fifth Avenue, I wondered why I'd gone to Atari in the first place. I was impatient, pure and simple. And it would be interesting to gain an inside view of the world of video gaming. The truth is that after my first conversation with a programmer, I spent nearly all my time there like some possessed video maniac trying to find a winning solution. There I was in the midst of the Warner Bros. of tomorrow, on site at perhaps the most fascinating industry in the world, maybe in history, running around from office to office like an idiot to nail down some particular little sequence of moves to practice so I could match what they said good players could do. I didn't call the engineering department to ask for a tour of the design facilities, but instead with, "Sorry to bother you, but I forgot whether you said you thought the first or second brick from the left was a better choice?" God knows what they made of me.

I'd gone to Atari and spoken to programmers. I figured that since these games are "programmed" after all, as most of us know without the slightest idea what that really means, myself included, "programmers" should know about them. And they do. They know all about how these microworld events are organized. Had I asked them how to actually learn to get good, asked them about high scores at the game, and left it at that, things would've been different. But they were programmers, not coaches, and it was quite natural they'd lay things out as they did, with the angles, and strategies, and all. Besides, I asked for that, asked how to win, not how to learn. I should've known better than to go to a linguist for advice on how to acquire a language. Those good at describing structure are notoriously bad when it comes to teaching. They forget the action itself, enamored as they are with elegant reasoning.

Never having given even the slightest thought to what a program was, as soon as I heard about how the whole thing was put together I was grabbed by the image of a gridded playing field of invisible lines. I never figured the ball moved like a real ball, bending and swaying in the breeze. But the picture of these strictly determined paths hadn't ever occurred to me. I didn't give any thought at all to this aspect of the object. There was a paddle, and a ball, and the task was to hit away this barricade, pure and simple. The new vision thoroughly recast how I began to see the screen. There'd only been an opponent because I wasn't in command of the routes, had simply let *Breakout* do things to me while fighting back the best I could without knowing the organization of its ways and whereabouts. Now I imagined an intrinsic elegance in sitting back watching a TV, systematically directing the patterned unfolding of its sights in a precisely detailed way, moving through a switchyard of invisible tracks. That seemed far more exciting than a contest with a contraption that simply has speed, endurance, and the capacity to do more things than you could handle at once in its favor. What's the point in racing a sewing machine to see who can do a hem faster? Little did I know both how much and how little you could just sit back.

There I was on the Atari premises, and here were these rather speedy and excited young guys and gals in jeans and sneakers with Rembrandt prints and psychedelic posters in their offices, pianos and guitars lying about, Bartok coming out of this room, the Stones out of that, more TV sets going at once than in ten Sears Roebucks put together, more technology and color and instruments and charts and sounds and knobs and controls and computers of every conceivable description than you'd ever see under one roof outside Silicon Valley, programmers literally sleeping in vans in the parking lot so they'd stay close to their consoles. And with the enthusiasm and animation any corporate manager would give away his American Express card for, they're laying out the lovely little grammars of these microworlds for me, speaking with such expertise and command and exhilaration, so as we went through the rundown of strategies and angles and hints I figured myself in the presence of an artist's colony of the first magnitude, Black Mountain of the eighties, everyone working their brains off, chip monks chipping away colors, movements, and sounds into a whole marvelous assortment of new instruments. After a fifteen-year dose of the tube, these young programmers were going to take charge of what prime time could really mean. What I overlooked was that it was a business enterprise first and foremost, not an aesthetic monastery. And prime time is mighty expensive. It ain't good business to let players quickly gain consistency with a winning video game pattern, at least not yet, not without some modifications, not without getting rid of some of the contest and its profitable organization. It's okay to get good fast, but only if the action is so organized that once you do you don't get bored. But why rock the boat; who in his right mind doesn't run with a winning horse? There's lots of loose change in the world.

Hey, I wanna play one of these things too. Getting the lowdown on *Breakout* felt almost like the first time somebody told me a few rules about how to produce some chords to harmonize a melody on the piano, at the age of sixteen, and I'd rushed home with the clue to a big part of my future. There's perhaps a time in the learning of every form of activity when the notion that the events are governed by rules gives you sudden access to at least a way into things, however misguided that idea may be. Oh, yeah, no kidding, you can substitute a dominant seventh chord on the flatted second, hit the fast slam before the eighth shot, one ball all the way, just on one side, down to a thin strip of blue and then scoot the rectangle across the screen step by step? You mean it's got that much order and finesse to it? All right, MIT jazz, here I come. Little did I know you had to snap your synapses instead of your fingers. Little did I know that you can't beat the house when it controls the odds, when it controls what skills are and whether they can or can't be learned by repetition, when it designs the game so that the only order in which you can learn is the order that it'll teach you to learn, at twenty-five cents a throw. I'd completely lost sight of the most vital fact—that *Breakout* was an arcade game in its original form, and all the essential features of this elegant neuroeconomic object had been preserved in the home version.

For all I knew at the time, I was about to beat the thing, had the key to the puzzle, and since I counted on my ability and motivation to practice sequences of movement to perfection, expertise was within sight. I had the recipe. The rest was just learning how to cook. All questions of aesthetics aside, I'd be lying not to admit some showing-off fantasies. Wait 'til Herb and Paul can see what I can do. Beating them on brute determination would be one thing, but pulling a neat little pattern on them in a game that appeared so patternless in many respects, not laid out in the sort of territory where we traditionally expect a "puzzle" to reside, like in a *Pac-Man* maze for instance—beating them that way was something else. I could see the makings for a good hustle, now that I knew about the invisible rows and columns along which the numerically switched lights seemed to move. So what if the joke you so casually pull out of the hat from this endless stockpile at instant command was told to you that morning and is the only one you remember?

The moment I figured out my opening, took a first ball a long way down the line, and could thus see for myself the power that understanding the program promised, I was hooked on perfection. I had a good opening sequence, and I'd work it over until it was down pat. Then I'd discover the next shots in the sequence as I went along, and I'd work them out too. From the looks of things, seeing how fast that opening was identified and seeing I could reproduce it pretty quickly the first day, I couldn't wait to get the whole thing down perfect. As soon as I found my pattern I called the *Super Breakout* programmer. "How much of the game is solved once you've got the opening?" "About a third," he said, "another third is returning the shot whenever it comes back down through the hole, and the final third is dealing with the ending." They calculate everything.

I was turned on to *Breakout* in an altogether new way, and that held the most peculiar sorts of costs in store—fifty hours of torture for one thing. The analogy to a melody, a particularly paced sequence of particularly located steps to be mastered as all intricate gestural skills are mastered, by practicing the movements—how could that not fit here? It couldn't fit for the simple reason I was in the presence of an altogether new creature, this video game. The objects and events on the screen, the entire organization of the human being squared off against it, the whole kit and caboodle lies in its own mysterious turf. What is a "thing" in this terrain, what does an event mean here, what could "skill" be with these events, what, if anything, do the notions of movement, coordination, thought, action, emotion, consciousness, motivation, and a "nervous system" refer to with respect to this new microworld in our midst? Movements don't look or feel like movements, skill doesn't feel like skill, and learning to do well requires a sort of mute commitment to a schedule that will bring you before the events of the game with your tongue hanging out and a quarter in your hand, as the condition under which you're to live with the thing for a while in order to come upon the way to competence, as the only way to come upon competence. It was a very well-programmed profit maker and it had to be analyzed on its own terms. Analogies from the solid world were altogether inappropriate. If you want to play melodies, buy a piano. If you want to get good at *Breakout,* you've got to pay. The home model you pay for all at once? Some confusion here, a bit of cultural lag, a commodity in the midst of uncertain neuroeconomic evolution.

I had all the facility I needed to do my five-shot sequence as soon as I'd done it a couple of times. What I mean to say is I found no appreciable difference between how it felt to do it the first time and how it felt on the last. No sense of a developing command. Every time I picked up the knob it felt the same way as the day I bought it. And my inconsistencies had very little if anything to do with me in particular. My reflexes, so-called, are as good as the next guy's, my eyesight is fine, my hands steady, nerves no worse off than most. And I know how to "concentrate" perfectly well. I'd concentrated like crazy for fifty hours that were worse than cramming all night for a calculus test when you forgot what a "limit" meant, figuring you'd put off studying for that course until the night before the final since you had a knack with math and really cared more about Nietzsche or girls that semester. I concentrated like crazy on exactly the wrong thing. And if you are new at video games and after twenty hours at *Breakout* take the reset switch in hand and set yourself the task of hitting those five shots consistently, a dozen times in a row, say, whenever you come to the machine, you'll have the same trouble I did, trying to think your way out of something you can't get out of that way, practicing over and over again so you can get it right when you have it right all along and all you're getting to happen is an inconsistency that'll give you something to work on. I had all the skills to do my five-shot sequence the first time I did it, and while I figured understanding the program was the trick, it was following it that really mattered.

There was a limit as to how much I could take of that reset switch after all. Damned if I'm going to put in another fifty hours like the last. If that switch was a purposefully designed functional equivalent to the arcade quarter cycle, fooling you into wrongly figuring you can practice little pieces to get better so you'll put in more time at the thing because otherwise, since it was "free," you might get too good and too bored too fast—if that was its actual intent they were mighty clever folks. Or perhaps they were mighty stupid, and figured if consumers have a reset option they'll conquer a game faster and buy more cartridges. A deeply interesting commodity these video games, havens for a truly refined marketing phenomenology.

Then what was the missing ingredient? Say I played my opening correctly, broke through as planned, and could then place the ball back up through the slot whenever it came down, a "much easier" task then the first five shots. I could then take the single serve a long way toward the finish. That happened from the beginning when I'd first learned the order back in the motel in California. So say I played the opening right, went a long way with one ball, and then missed a shot. A dozen bricks were left, something like that. Whenever I hit the reset switch under the energy supplied by that near success, whenever a new first serve followed quickly on the end of such a run, there was an excellent chance the five-shot opening would go well again. Getting away from the machine and gaining some distance, I now clearly saw that the one factor, one variable, one thing that could most increase consistency on a next trial, would be to get the opening right and go all the way toward the end. Not taking a nap or a long walk. And two days away from the game hadn't made the slightest difference. Everything I explicitly try to do sometimes works and just as often fails. If I get the five shots right and then immediately hit the reset lever without playing further along, ridiculously keeping tally of successive repetitions, the chance of success on the next trial is if anything lessened. Almost the opposite of what repetition brings with a true skill. But right on the heels of a good long run toward the end, I hit the switch in the right spirit, keyed up with some sort of adrenalinized solidity that automatically wipes clean all analytic reason as my thoughts and look snap out of the "five shot" mode like a near-miss collision wipes out everything else. And I get the opening right once again. Two or three times in a row, almost always, in that context. The seduction of a nearly elegant one-ball sweep cycles me back into the next trial with a solid pulse, not in the movements, for as we've seen that kind has no bearing, but in the veins, throbbing me right up there somewhere near terror, mobilizing a sort of immobility of the body so none of its manifest natural movements can rhythmically interfere with the arrhythmic sequence. The excitement of a possibly winning finish creates a way of being that prevails over caution, or indifference, or confident assertiveness or any of the other sorts of moods I can at least try to get underway, change, or let go of with sentences. It wells up from a place somewhere down underneath just plain "caring." And then, as on many occasions before, successful play only lasts for a little while because the kick tapers off.

Things always fell off after a couple of runs because there was no progress. I was a long way from being able to take one ball the full route and hadn't the faintest idea how to make things better. My endings were far from ideal. I got down to a dozen or so bricks whose haphazard arrangement made it perfectly obvious other shots had to be figured out if the promised one-ball clearing was to happen. From the outset I knew my opening was only part of the solution, but at first I figured I'd deal with details later. I didn't know how many shots had to be worked on, didn't know where the most critical decisions lay. And in any case, the programmer said one was a third of the way through when the opening was settled. But now the disheveled appearance of my endings increasingly told me there was much more to the puzzle than the first bunch of targets. It looked messy, but I just couldn't see how or why.

To take just one example, slightly different ways to field the slam shot, sixth in my sequence, had varying consequences that didn't make themselves known till much farther down the line. I could see that without being able to see the details. Handling this shot's return one way, the breakthrough slice had one pattern, while handled otherwise the corridor came out just a little bit differently. As far as just breaking through was concerned, these variations didn't always matter, but it was apparent that over the long run the precise eventual arrangement of bricks depended in part on this sixth shot's placement. And of course on all other shots along the way. For all I could tell just looking at things, it might be the sixth shot was especially crucial for how the last three bricks were arranged on screen, or the last two, or last seven. Who could know? There was no way to visualize the whole all at once. I'd come upon my pattern in an hour by trying this and that, assembling it together as a piece, going back and forth till it was born. You had to do it that way, couldn't decide on a particular order of bricks out of context of everything else it would entail. So for all I knew in principle, while my opening might've been good enough to get me to the slam in time, and good enough to get me most of the way down, it might've been altogether mistaken in a one-ball strategy. But I'd been impatient. They said avoid the deflection shot, so I'd avoided the deflection shot. They said go up one side of the corridor, so I went up one side of the corridor. And so far as I could tell I was on the right track. No sooner did I have my opening than I could go a long distance with one ball. So who could ask for more? It never even occurred to me that just because they told me properties, of a good opening solution didn't necessarily mean that any solution with those properties would do the job. And I'd ignored how little the manufacturer would make if things were as simple as they looked.

I couldn't begin to see what to do to make things better at the end because I spent such little time just hanging around there to watch the looks of the finish from the standpoint of a one ball strategy. So I'd get to the end in more or less the same shape several times in a row whenever I played out a correct opening sequence, and then I lost interest. Just a touch. A touch was taken off the intensity and striving, and on the next trial my sequence was a touch off base. After two or three unmethodical and therefore unsuccessful attempts to make a next run better, my determination waned a bit. The following run suffered on some minute critical level as the motivating pulse subsided, I'd make a mistake, and then cycle back into the repair process where I foolishly spent more of my time. A vicious cycle, a recurring downward spiraling inability of my play to remotivate itself.

I stayed at the beginning practicing movements for how to get somewhere, while I should've been playing the game from front to back as was intended. I should've used as many of the five balls as it took to clear the screen, keeping score by one or another of the offered options, or having a contest. I should've behaved no differently than if it cost a quarter to start up again each time. Success was only possible when you played as if you were in an arcade and didn't want to thoroughly squander your money, not without making sure there was more loose change to get your hands on, enough left over for lunch or to take a cab home or get one more martini at the airport. I stayed at the beginning practicing movements instead of staying tied into the economic structure of the game, which is to say its program, so that I'd be brought to unlock its secrets in the only way they can be unlocked: bit by bit, piecing together an eventual winning sequence by working from both ends toward the middle while always cycling from front to back, always drawn toward a next higher level so the motivation stays way up there to permit more consistent passes over sequences of potentially good moves. In other words, profitably. To care in the right way you must submit to those stimulations encountered when the full game is played from front to finish. Cut yourself off from these, go for consistency with techniques that work elsewhere, step outside the scheduled front to back way of learning on which the game's program and profit depend, and you'll fail. You'd have to play according to the rules, where the object is to eliminate all the bricks from the screen, period, with no resetting and starting over. I'd actually gotten into bad habits before I went to Atari, never really respecting the structure of the game, never scoring the action, hitting the reset button indiscriminately almost right from the outset at Herb's house, happily panning away while the world blew up. Where did I come off figuring you could improvise your way through a nuclear war?

It began to dawn on me. The central skills of these games arise out of lucratively programmed caring. Competence is possible only when action is motivated in those ways the game itself motivates it, and the game motivates action in ways proven to be most profitable in a rapid coin turnover scheme. That makes the skills inseparable from the profitably arranged enticements that bring them into being. It's not that you have to "care" in order to get good, but rather that you have to be kept caring. You've got to be kept in the right state so you'll get to some places a little bit better all the time, so that a goal remains alive by always moving just ahead out of reach and you keep wanting to attain it without having to spend a fortune. You don't have to figure out how to do that. You can't. The way to be kept caring is most delicately built right into the program, so long as you don't mess with your freedoms, don't get hooked on the reset button or reckless with your quarters. Do that and it gets harder to be kept caring. By no means is this the only way we know to motivate ourselves to do something again and again till we succeed. But it's the only way to sustain the lucratively programmed caring needed to master these current generation video games. The altogether remarkable fact about this little cultural artifact is that the learning curves of the skills, hence their very nature, and the incitements to play the game, these were engineered as two sides of the same coin. A quarter.

Of course what I'd wanted before I came to Atari, to reach a handful of bricks with a serve left to go, a slow lob that'd be easy to handle—that couldn't have mattered less anymore. This sort of ending was always now had whenever I carried one shot through as planned, but I never even bothered taking the next serve to wipe off the screen. You're in a dangerous and frantic situation, it's too much to handle, so you simplify things to bring it under control. But once you accomplish that, it loses all its attractiveness. It was cutting the intensity of a crazy ending, not really trying to win, that had motivated my desire to attack fast bricks early. So it was an incorrectly motivated strategy, a sign I'd already pulled back from the intended use of the game. I could see that now, for this "solution" canceled out the excitement inspiring it, and the remaining slow bricks on screen were now just so many illuminated rectangles devoid of all neuroemotional significance.

If the game could be mastered with as little time as I'd put into it, it wouldn't have existed. But the guy said a "third" of the way? Looking back now, I suppose he assumed I was talking of a proven opening, and that what he meant by these proportions had to do with the minor skill of handling the shots, not the major accomplishment of discovering them. Either that, or he was looking down on some sort of overall decision-making phases of the program. In any event, I'd inadvertently put myself in a no-win situation. With a "solution" of the sort I had, based on principles rather than experience, practiced for perfection to the exclusion of all other possibilities under an aesthetic ideal rather than to win, I was worse off than with no "solution" at all. While my opening might not have had any longer term worth, in its way it's too good for me at this stage. Insisting on a one-ball solution before I'm in any position to really suppose I have one, I wind up with a configuration toward the end that's neither here nor there, can't possibly improve, and yet without progress I can't motivate frequent enough correct trials to detect precise sequences of steps down the line. Successful pattern detection, that lucratively programmed visual calculating rather than motorific facility making up the true skill of video gaming, clearly involves seeing pattern all over, not just from some idealized starting point step by step to a finish on the hope it'd work out well after all.

The whole trouble arose out of a misunderstanding. And a reset option. I'd mistakenly heard the description of a "good game" as a set of instructions for how to learn, rather than a general characterization of the sort of result one could hope to attain playing *Breakout* a lot in the right sort of overall context. They didn't tell me how good solutions were acquired, and I didn't ask. They told me how the program worked. But not entirely. They left out something. In their enthusiasm to explain its inner elegance, they didn't tell me the program specifically evolved for playing front to back without starting again if you don't like how it goes.

I can't get my five shots consistently, but it's clear they didn't explicitly set things up that way. How in the world could you possibly design it so you'd get a sequence of moves perfectly sometimes, right from the start, but be unable to reliably reproduce it? Play around with the ball's speed, paddle size, dimensions of the barricade, say, trying to organize a strip of action that'll happen just perfectly but only now and then? Not a chance. My inconsistency arises from a lack of that sort of properly generated caring that only the fully played game itself arouses, that freshly invented electroneurologically incited want that obliterates analytic thought here. So just as you've got to work out a pattern by building it up from front to finish and finish to front, they likewise had to have designed the game by fiddling around with all its features simultaneously, while testing it in a context of enforced front to back, highly motivated play, constantly adjusting things from every side to get just the right commodity. The inconsistency that I encountered never had to occur to them, since the game wasn't tested with the reset switch, but with a quarter.

Walking through Times Square, I passed these huge video arcades, where during the daytime young businesspeople come over from the East Side during their lunch hours and stand next to unemployed black teen-agers at adjacent Pac-M*e*n. The industry was democratizing inter-neighborhood social mobility at perhaps the most classless public places in town. Where else in the city but in front of adjacent video games will you find white guys in three-piece suits alongside kids from Harlem? At urinals in Yankee Stadium maybe, waiting for a light to change at certain border intersections, but never for an hour, both doing the same thing, both losing quarters at the same rate. Now that's what I call good business.

Watching the frenzy, I imagined the place as a marketing lab for *Breakout*. Like a jerk I hadn't inquired about what went into designing and testing arcade games in the industry. But the whole thing now seemed perfectly obvious. The object itself held all the clues to the method of its invention. As for the nature of the game's events and what "highly motivated" means in their context, what possible analogy could you use from the marketing psychology of solid world consumption and value? Three-piece suiters and the poor, kids and adults, side by side, spending at the same rate for the same action? That's like inventing oxygen.

Like all arcade or adapted arcade forms in this first generation of electrical creatures, *Breakout* emerged from the decision to implant interactive video commodities into the world via coin-op financing. Say I'm a computer programmer, and I've just rented this huge space in Times Square. Thousands pass every minute, trillions of nerve endings walking by. In the back room I've managed to get what looks like a ball on the screen. Technology has emerged to where you could light up small portions of a TV. There are these thousands of tiny light bulbs, a switch controlling each one, and the system of switches is routed through a fast adding machine called a computer. Just a whole lot more in a small space with much quicker current. Forty years ago, millions watched light bulbs go on and off to electrically flash the news of Pearl Harbor right down the block along the side of what was the New York Times building. Giant precursors to the word processor, these wire services in the sky. Bet they made the war more exciting.

Now things were miniaturized, that's all. Fast-moving folks, those Japanese.

So I've made a little dab, one hundred tiny light bulbs square, a third of an inch swatch that looks like a ball when I make it move with instructions that turn off all of one set of switches and then turn on a bunch more for bulbs close by, superfast, one swatch after another after another, "moving" in straight lines let's say, coming from various areas of the top of the screen down at varying angles toward the bottom. Well, that's kind of neat. Now what do I do? I could make all sorts of shapes, I suppose, have them come from different directions to create a little world of moving lights that'd be fun to look at. But I'm not sure if and how they'll pay for that, and more importantly, the instructions would get very complicated and my computer isn't big enough. Someday, perhaps. But for now, since I've got a thing that looks like a ball, maybe I can hit it. Put a switch in my hand and let me control the sights in real time, math time.

I can store instructions, hold them electrically alive in a thing I'll call a "memory." Ooooh yeah, "memory," sounds mysterious, makes my electronic switchyard seem intelligent. That'll sell. If I can show extraordinary-looking things with my machine, I'll bet philosophers and scientists will even try to rethink "memory" into something made up of stored coded instructions for switching routines. They'll even think this memorizer is like a brain if it does a lot of things that even look on the surface like what brains think brains do. They can make their quarters with theories about artificial intelligence, while other philosophers will make theirs arguing about what "intelligence really means," how it's something very different from computer memory, how artificial intelligence is altogether artificial. As for me, I'm a practical man in business, the rent here is outrageous, and this computer cost me a fortune. If my machine stimulates vital controversy on the nature of man and intelligence, focuses a sharply pinpointed interest in the relation between freedom and technology, so much the better. Memory. Yeah. I like it. Just the right image for the times since we keep forgetting the past, things change so quickly these days, and there's just too much to remember.

I make an implement, lighting up a thin rectangle of light bulbs along the bottom of the screen, and it looks like a paddle, and I can control it from the outside while storing instructions for the ball inside. When the ball circuits approach the paddle coordinates, just when it looks like the lights touch, the circuits are then instructed back up. It's wild. Sit there with a knob and it looks like I'm hitting something. It feels different, but looks like that. I'll call it a game. After all, I've got to tie my invention to the social structure, and making the action look like other kinds of action, on the surface at least, I can legitimate it, give it those characteristics needed to fit it into an available slot in a culture, and thereby in the personal budget. Maybe someday it'll evolve into an educational resource, remedy, religious icon, household decoration, companion, or a form of meditation and therapy. God only knows. The market and culture will decide.

The neighborhood has a sort of concretized county fair atmosphere, people strolling to and fro with loose change. Three balls for a quarter and win your baby a doll, your doll a baby. That's a good model at first since I can't sell them these things to take home. They won't go for it, not yet. It'd cost a fortune. You've got to have "lots going on" before people spend lots of money these days. I suppose I could someday organize a performance, charge admission, and have people watch the thing in use. But in its current state, especially with this small TV screen, I'll have to make it on individual players. What do they win here? Who knows. For one thing it sure ain't the prize that makes guys put up quarters at a county fair. And if I'm getting off on this action perhaps they will too. How to speak of the rewards? I'll leave that to the P.R. department. And to the society. The first question is: Will it work? Put a coin collector on the machine, and give them three balls for a quarter.

Best I can tell sitting here playing with the thing, it feels to me like you lose interest if it's too hard, and if it's too easy I won't make a penny. I could make it so difficult you'd need lots of time and quarters to make progress, but then I'll probably need someone who's really good out there in the front room as a role model to prove learning is possible. Maybe someday we'll make kids play the game like we once made them practice the piano or do homework, someday when this gaming gets super-respectable, gets the rep chess has, say, is seen good for the human spirit, a route to familiarity with computers in general. But given what I've got, for the while I'll take my bet on more immediate enticement with short-term success and failure at the action. An action game.

I arrive at a paddle size and speed that seems right. Got to space those dolls a certain distance apart so only one guy in ten gets his baby one while everybody else sees it happen. The rent's due soon, no time for fancy theorizing, so I rush to settle on a first shot at things. I've got it where it takes a while to hit the ball consistently, and yet you have some success right off. But I can't really tell anymore since I've been at this thing for months, don't know whether it's the paddle size or the ball speed that makes for more difficulty. I need subjects. I know, I'll set up each machine a little differently and put on a counter that keeps track of the quarters. Straightforward marketing. Nielsen ratings. And I've got the computer right in the back room. Add things up to find out the paces and places where the action is.

How do you like that? First day of business and I've made a couple of hundred bucks. Not good, not in this location, but not that bad. Machine number six did best.

I'll program them all like version six for tomorrow. Next day, three times the income. Holy chip. It seems as if this paddle-size–ball-rate combination holds them for about twenty minutes, and seems that every time a player misses the third ball he gets a little angry, or something like that. I watch the hand go into the pocket with vengeance. I've tapped into something. Maybe it's a sort of perceptual incongruity, a universal human need for closure. A near miss upsets the balance of some gestalt within the system. Who knows? I haven't the faintest idea what's really going on, why it works, how these altogether newly synthesized events on screen pass right into the "nervous system," getting the hand to dip into the pocket. How could I? Does anybody really truly know why people spend money, even with traditional "entertainments"? Of course not. It works, that's all. Pure praxis. They seem to be having a good time, and number six machine is earning a few bucks an hour.

But I do some calculation in the back room, figuring out the rent, the cost of machines, the number of passersby at twenty minutes each for a buck, and I'm in trouble. What happens in the winter when it's freezing, and how many Times Squares are there anyhow? If the same people come back day after day that'd be one thing, but I notice there are no repeaters, which means as things now stand I'll need a constant turnover of customers, or should I call them "players," or "fans."

Users. They use the thing. User friendly computers. I use, do you?

I've got to keep the same user at the game for a longer time, bring that user back again and again, and make it harder so he can't last too long on the same quarter while at the same time he'll keep wanting to play. I increase the speed of the ball, but find there's little problem keeping up, until you just reach a limit and start going nuts. Nobody's going to let themselves be continuously wound up, the "tension," whatever it is, has to level off, and yet somehow it doesn't look like the sort of skill I can easily enrich. Oddly enough, manipulations of the paddle size, ball speed, and angles don't substantially increase difficulty, and I can't seem to really make hitting the ball an ultrarefined task, like batting a fast baseball pitch or threading a needle. Initial results on machine six were too crude, for while I know how to establish a mildly difficult opening, beyond there I'm stuck.

A surprise element. They go along for ten hits and suddenly the ball shoots down to throw them off guard. I put in a slam shot, run a bunch of quarter tests to pick a good speed, and find they stay a little while longer. But I notice something more subtle. Before, players didn't spend the whole twenty minutes learning, for in about five they got the hang of it. Yet during the rest of the time nobody handled the ball continuously, and I made my quarters off their "foolish errors," "lapses in attention," whatever it was. Now when they first see the slam and put in a quarter to go again, they suddenly handle earlier slow play better. The slam adds a "thrill" to the game: Their hands go into their pockets a bit more heatedly, I hear them curse at times when they miss, watch intensity grow as they near shot ten. But it's not really earning more. I need other elements to profitably increase difficulty.

Five years later I've got *Breakout*. I made computer inventions to increase my yield, as others did likewise. The technology sprouted on every rational front, from every sector of the speedy economy, and the creature evolved through complex interaction between resources for experimentation, quarters for expenditure, and the nature of the so-called nervous system. Without the search for microprocessors to define effective accounting in small business for instance, the machine wouldn't have been chipped down to its present size, down to where I could put all these colors, sounds, and paddle angles into a portable if somewhat heavy object. Out of a multifaceted process of invention stimulated by interests throughout a society obsessed with creating, gathering, and analyzing "information," programming techniques and computer hardware had evolved so that more and more differentiated aspects of a TV signal could be instructed. And it turned out that the object was elaborated by adding more visual elements to the field.

For example, I instructed a barricade, gave users a target for the ball, and evoked a game concept: eliminate the wall. I suppose I could've had it instead where hitting things became a more intricately mobile affair, could've made the alignment of objects a much more delicate manual achievement. But that would've involved an altogether different style of programming. The resolution of the TV screen would've had to substantially increase for dexterity of movement to be required in the flattened two-dimensional space. The paddle would've had to be subdivided into dozens of angles, and the interfacing equipment would've needed heftier calibration. But for a bunch of reasons that only a cultural, economic, and psychological investigation of endless depth could unravel, the thrust of developments led toward increasing the complexity of the sight, not the tactile nature of the interface. Switching programs, the on/off quality of these lights, and the interests to which the computer was being addressed, this all led to the creation of discrete, episodic, instantaneously timed, rapidly paced, scorable actions, exploiting the inherently polarized binary guts of the lickety-split machine. I could use the same knob and ball, and now found out, quite by chance through real live trials since there was no model to draw upon, that the game could be made more profitable through the construction of obstacles, bunches of lights that would pounce on and off by numerical cue, a field of impactful events, objectives, encumbrances, and impediments in which the simple coordinating skills of hitting the ball could be situated. After all, button pushing was intrinsic to the logic, charm, and power of the medium. If you want intricate fingerings, take up the guitar or needlepoint. Here most of you stays quite put in front of a small TV screen as you play sights with understanding eyes.

So I instructed a barricade, had a readily recognizable game theme and objective, and now began to coin a new commodity. Each and every feature of the product was the experimentally arrived-at consequence of a worth it generated for itself in relation to every other feature, a quarter at a time. Precisely engineered to maximize profits, it was a "game" whose entire internal structure was calculated to both establish and respond to the value for a coin. No different in this respect from many products. But what an extraordinarily pure instance of the very essence of a commodity, this pay-as-you-learn-to-hold-on-to-the-action object, this programmed learning device with increments of knowledge and motivation to learn laid on two bits by two bits at a time.

I had a barricade, and a paddle, and fiddled with the program to find an engagingly costly way for the user to eliminate it. Put in twenty bricks and these particular angles and you earn this much, put in forty and change the angles and the yield is different, put in sixty and you earn less at first but more over the long run. Because of delicate and mysterious relations between features of the barricade and varying rates of progress at different stages of play, decisions about parameters reflected the entire sociological context of the game's situation and use among quarter holders. For one thing, it happened that the turnover rate significantly mattered. They got better at it the longer they stayed. That was partially planned, for once you had a "game" you had to allow some sort of competence. But improvement was also the unanticipated result of those very features designed to make things harder, as in the case of the slam. Jack up the ball speed to make for a more hazardous course of surprises, and that "tension" at the same time figures into the incitement needed to consistently motivate earlier tasks. So there were trade-offs at every point. Can't have everything. When located where the self-same players had repeated access to the object with few casual users on the scene, a game's intake rapidly declined. Paddle angles, barricade composition, ball speed, and a host of other features were all adjusted to norms about typical user patterns and typical gaming locations. In some places they'd do wonderfully, in others terribly, and you had to strike a midpoint somewhere in between.

A hit and miss proposition with no solid theory to go on, making any detailed account of why a game made money impossible. All one could hope and search for were ways of talking about desired attributes that produced rough principles useful for contriving a promising format. It somehow seemed to work to make up various apparent "levels" marked by what looked like "dramatic new events." It seemed to work for the action to be paced at a certain rate. It seemed to work to encourage "holding on" while simultaneously attending a slightly overwhelming set of obstacles. But beyond such roughshod and slippery concepts, actual details of the format arose through trial and error experimentation as the object discovered a worth for itself.

As the competition got involved, new games emerged, reported high earnings, and the effort was made to replicate their productive features. Sounds and colors were shown to somehow increase the yield, for instance. For one thing, they seemed to attract new players. For another, the more coloration a game had, the more it looked like players would pay to play without making rapid progress, so difficulty could rise a bit to increase profits in the early stages of use before improvement substantially reduced the hourly flow. For still another, an increase in the sheer extent of material on screen added to the neuroemotional significance of a near miss. The scene invitingly quivered with temptation. But again, the trade-offs. The highly pitched and rapidly excited sounds of fast action pulled quarters out of pockets, but also aided a user's capacity to rhythmically incorporate the shift from slow to slam action, for instance.

From a pure business standpoint, an object that remains profitable at the same rate in a coin-op economy no matter how long a single user stays with it—that's one heck of an ingenious invention. But this game, designed for skill rather than luck, was situated in settings frequented by minors, and had to be masterable to legitimate itself. It's not that people won't spend quarters for action leading "nowhere," and lots of them at that. Witness a gambling casino. Witness drugs. But there were social limitations on the direction in which the commodity could go and still receive wide currency. Most important, however, the possibility of mastery for all quarter practical purposes was an unavoidable consequence of the very nature of the object as it had experimentally evolved.

For it was indeed a game, an extraordinarily elegant one at that, and no matter how much one sought to circumvent a contest, there was no getting around that fact. As a player, I'd just picked the wrong skills to work on, that's all, worrying about my gesture instead of the looks of things. A set of obstacles was created. A pace of action was established. A mode of front to back play was engineered into the machine, reset button notwithstanding, so you had to negotiate through the field without missing, getting bumped over, having your lights switched off on you because you ran into the wrong numbers. The central skill of video gaming was orchestrated out of continuous trial and error market testing: a sufficiently dense texture of routes through the TV neighborhood was set up in conjunction with a fixed, manageable, yet somewhat frantic pace for exciting travel. Each variable was economically adjusted till the setup reached the point where a typical user could only see a safer path through by traversing the territory again and again and again, often enough seeing a bit more and thereby getting a bit more action for a quarter, that he'd want to get still more again. Loose change in the pockets of human bodies, and the most rationalized piece of machinery since the wheel, interacted back and forth over many variations until a new creature was born: a real time, front to back, self-contained and scheduled sleight of hand magic trick chip.

Say you're in a car on an LA freeway. The accelerator isn't under your control. It's altogether easy to steer around on readily negotiated tracks. But the problem is these on ramps and off ramps, dividers, barricades, and traffic appearing from every which direction, and if you could only slow things down, you could see what's going on, if you could only get on top or inside the thing or get a map to perceive the whole all at once so you could figure out how to get through the maze to that exit over there to the left, uh-oh it just went by again, maybe it's this ramp, no the other, no, that one, no, there's that truck again and I can't yet tell where it comes from. *Wap*.

EYELIGHTS

WITH EVERYTHING SAID AND DONE, when I turn the game on back at the hotel and the first serve comes from the corner with randomness in my favor, I still can't resist going for my opening or whatever you want to call it. Maybe it's permanently stuck in my brain. Neuro-tic fixation. The first two shots are correct, you could say, and then I miss, of course, hitting the ball with the center of the paddle or something like that, so the third return goes too far right screen. But this time I'll play it out anyhow, with no resetting, and when it comes down, I manage to pitch it back up to the left, surprised to then find I can still reach a slam brick before the deflection.

How do you like that. I'm right back into efficacious play, now planfully improvising a route by turning what looked like a mistake into an alternative way to go, using the quick breakthrough strategy as a guiding policy you can realize in varying alternative ways. So the clues didn't hurt after all, had I only done this sort of thing with them from the start, treated them as general maxims rather than strict rules for building one specific solution. Slam, it comes down, I again miss a placement and the ball goes to the right once more. Yet why not play this side for a while. Then during a third shot to that far corner I shift the paddle just a notch as the ball is rising toward the barricade, so on the downfall I can pitch it back left again and still maintain a basically sound approach. The strong tendency is always to hit with the paddle's leading half, so when the ball comes down from one side you unselfconsciously return it that same way. But switchovers take an unnatural alignment that must be thoughtfully prepared, can't occur to you at the last second. As the fast ball goes to one side you've got to be set for a change in advance, can't shift your paddle once it's midair. With no acceleration to latch on to in course and no time and space for any last-minute realignments, pulling off such a switchback signals a new structural understanding of how the attack can be channeled.

Two more shots now and I've broken through, still on one ball, and to tell the truth I don't see the least bit of damage done by the slight mess I've made. At least I'm into play rather than unproductive practice, committing myself to the game in a way that'll motivate me toward the end. And as I near the finish properly driven toward the goal, maybe I'll then care enough to see the consequence of that nick on the right side, gain insight into the real import of a clean opening and not just its theory. Insight. That's the trick. Such little movement happens on the surface.

I'm learning to "control the ball." Yes and no. I'm learning to see promising destinations. Certainly a big part of any skill is knowing where you're going over and above the generic bodily facility to move about. If you want to do a disco step, you've got to appreciate where to take your feet, what the pattern is. Here it's just lopsided, that's all, very little needed on the dexterity side while everything hinges on seeing the hinges, understanding where and when to employ one's capacities. In ten hours you've got all the manual skills to do the *Breakout* ballet, and then spend your time trying to decipher how movements can be laid out in the thoroughly blueprinted neighborhood. If you care enough, if you want to win and don't get sidetracked like I did with that scale practicing nonsense, forgetting the numbers you're up against. Once you know where you can go and where it's worth going, getting there's no sweat. Just caring and nerves.

I managed that switchover not because I've now gained enhanced tactile facility at precise paddle placement. Achieving the appropriate alignment isn't at all experienced as a manually delicate operation, the unnatural backside presentation of the paddle not encountered as an awkward "movement." Rather, the new skill involves detecting previously unseen prospects for programmed action, and you're in shape to handle these maneuvers if you think out your route a step or two in advance. While explicit consciousness of subdivisions is disruptive rather than helpful, intelligent control of the paddle makes it now feel somewhat like a set of discrete switches rather than a continuous surface for hitting. To the extent you "feel" anything, that is.

I'll visually improvise through the game like I did before I got the lowdown, only now I'm a bit wise to these layouts, and as the ball moves along it appears I'm glimpsing a tracked-ness to things, seeing a linearity to the paths along which it travels. The calculating video look gradually comes into isomorphic correspondence with nodes of the program, the eye-hand connection geared in increasingly rational alignment with the graphic tracing of the numbers in a way eyes and hands have never before been cooperatively scheduled. And through a relatively passive yet analytic gaze, these triangles, trapezoids, and trapeziums are drawn in strictly even and instantaneously punctuated time into your eyeballs, geometrically tagging the hands along, coordinating you in neurological tandem with the program. A video neuron drafting table with you as the paper.

Perhaps our being is now further shaped by the very programming motions typing hands have learned. Calculating arises out of primordial properties of our prereflective bodily being: two symmetrical halves, ten fingers, eyes on a horizontal plane in relation to the ground, and a mouth that likes to count out loud. We count and count and count until we invent a numbering system, based on ten digits, and some years later, having long since lost sight of how that system originally related to our anatomy's way of seizing hold of the world, we use ten digits to type instructions directing electricity to outline our body's mathematics back at itself. And we're thus now incarnated in the coolest digital version of ourselves to ever come along, a self-actuating, glistening little creature under glass that we now and then poke at through wires.

My scale practice inadvertently amounted to something after all, for I got angle experience, got to more precisely see that there were these vectors. The ball comes down from the right and I've glanced at the left—glanced analysis sufficing, no true aiming in the deeper sense of things. So I pitch, no I switch it over, and it fulfills my hope, not quite definitely, not where I actually know which particular brick it'll hit. But the routes have been tightened up a bit. The ball's traverse has a vaguely predictable regularity, as if the slopes are faintly visible if you just look hard enough to take them out. A complex railway yard, a console of coupling switches in the central tower, trains coming in from all sides through a dense fog with little clearings here and there. If only they didn't move quite so fast.

I'd like to really see all the routes. Wish the ball left a little meteor trail. Wish Atari published a blueprint.

It'd be instructive if every so often the hint of a bunch of thin track lines flashed on for a second, throwing you into more conscious touch with the perceptual environment you face here. It'd be nice to see the underlying coordinates so as to elucidate an illusion I have. As the ball sets out on a long diagonal track across the screen, I follow it with the slightest little sway of a gesture somewhere in my body. My head bobs a bit or I lean into the shot just a trifle, and the ball's path correspondingly presents itself to me with the very slightest hint of a curvature, as if I've bent the mathematics in my favor. But the more I now regard the ball as the rippling reflection of a linear equation on an unseen graph, I abandon that swaying engagement with its pace that makes it a "moving object" for me. To the extent I'm brought to witness the spectacle as a programmed and spatially fixed affair, there's a sense in which the ball is no more in motion in relation to my body than are the contours of a photograph as they come into being in a darkroom developing tray I now and then rock a bit so as to keep the solution flowing.

Would it undercut or enhance fascination with the object if we were reminded of the method by which it's organized? Flash on some hidden routes now and then, flash on some colors that show the five paddle segments, give me all the resources I need to make the tasks of pattern detection an explicit focus of attention. Let me stay more in touch with the new experiences of problem solving in this world and don't let them go unnoticed because I get more wrapped up in winning than seeing how I learn to win. Why not say in the instruction booklet: "This is a game involving the capacity to become increasingly familiar with angles and trajectories, detecting the orderly way in which an apparently free-floating object is a formula. Playing it through again and again, you develop a geometrically directed and constantly paced way of seeing that will eventually incline you to transcend the illusion of objects in motion."

Farther down the line I find myself involved in switching the ball through a sequenced cross-screen pattern as a shifting triangle knocks out the bottom two rows of bricks. It results from returning each shot with the same leading edge, no thoughts of subdivisions needed. Just switch the ball, I suppose it's with the same segment each time, and the angles take off two rows of bricks in adjacent order like compulsively nibbled corn on the cob. Seems a decent enough way to play, this uniform attack that doesn't degrade the barricade in a messy way that'll show up later. And in any case it's fun. Strange I never noticed such possibilities before, never noticed ordered sequences of brick removal until I started on my opening. Now the sight is suddenly very definite for a brief while, and I'm employing the paddle as a switching device in ways I hadn't before. Seeing a possible sequence, I'll "keep it going," that instruction all I need to actually hold it alive, the hands unselfconsciously tagging right along with the eye's decision. In precise calculating control for the first time now—excepting the five-shot opening hardly worth mentioning again—I'm headed toward a long string of particular destinations. And with this pattern underway I can now accurately anticipate each specific next location. First entering the triangulation, I didn't know which particular brick would get hit, but once two or three adjacent ones got removed, the next targets were precisely seen for as long as ten or fifteen returns. Then the run disintegrated as the triangle broke up when one of its sides encountered a wall. But the object was mine for a while, I was doing the playing for a change, precisely managing a spate of action in that way that characterizes all competent conduct: knowing just where you're going and then going there. It's becoming an instrument. Instantaneously punctuated picture music. Supercerebral crystal clear Silicon Valley eye jazz.

Again a big change in the significance of "playing the game." I'm directing the ball just here and just there, playing the circuit breaker as I've wanted from the start, not that I knew it was that sort of tool. And it's improvised. I'm not following a scripted solution, but switching my way along with at least occasional spot-by-spot control, finding some precisely particular places to go in course till the object's capacity for calculation overwhelms mine. I can take an intended sequence of sights off the screen, and with more practice in this mode it'll clearly get where I can knowledgeably control many angles, where there's little vagueness about where I'm headed, where I'll be able to improvisationally plan varieties of patterned routes through the landscape.

Wait a minute. From the standpoint of the game's sophisticated mastery, you elegantly win by a rapid breakthrough and continuous return of the ball through the slot so bricks are knocked off from above. Here I go drifting from the game again, trying to make pretty geometric figures with the thing instead of submitting to the contest. But why should I go for a logical perfection that gives you much less to do beyond staying all nerved up to switch the ball back up top every now and then? Of course there's that endgame I've long forgotten, those fast lockups surely making for lots of action. And there's bound to be an element of special drama in the formally pleasing accomplishment of a logically best solution. Maybe that approach most satisfies the object's programmed essence. But wouldn't the efficiency kick be short-lived? With a fully worked out strategy wouldn't you barely have to look, since you know where you're going by rule and the mere gaze could suffice for handling the switches? Strategically best moves are ultimately reductive, tailoring participation down to its absolute minimum in keeping with the times, giving you "command" from afar and behind the scenes, so to speak, with nothing much to do.

Do I really care about winning by this point, about those points, the clock, what a "good player" can or can't do? Enough is enough already. I'm sure it's fun to play a game now and then. It'd be engaging to have a contest with the clock, or to go for points in a game with the kids. I know I could hold my own against anyone with moderate experience so long as I don't botch my opening too much beyond recovery of the sort I managed here. But there's nobody around, and to tell the truth I never really got into this thing to be an accomplished microathlete. It was that panning shot at missiles that got me started off in the first place, the psychedelectric action of it all, not winning the war. As for clearing the screen with one ball, best I can now tell that'd only come about in due course with lots more angle experience and the necessary contest or quarter shortage to motivate dedicated holding-on. And I cared more about the formal elegance of that one ball sweep than its power to make me a winner. Say I can do it a few times, experience that thrill, congratulate myself for diligence, and win a few bets. Then what?

Here I am alone in a pitch-black hotel room, a middle-aged man with some time to kill, getting ready to check out some jazz clubs in Greenwich Village, in possession of an early cretinous offering from a gold rush grab bag of tubey thingies coming our way from hundreds of decision-making puzzle peddlers through-out the new electric "entertainment" industry. And now instead of playing the game it's packaged up to be, I've gotten into more or less occupying myself by outlining invisible triangles across the screen of a TV doodling machine. What am I doing?

Is it a game, puzzle, electronic pencil and paper, learning device, "brown study" kit, new form of worry beads, childish toy, the perceptual psychologist's most perfect incongruity tool, or a first immature token for what could one day be a significant means of rationalized artistic expression? You think *The Well-Tempered Clavier* is an ultimate embodiment of the aesthetic potentials mathematics can create? Computerized instruments can make the piano look like a set of bongos. These games got put into the world to get quarters, designed to generate interest to a passerby. But now you've gone out and bought one, set aside funds for that, made a decision about something a bit more than how to handle loose change and a few passing moments.

The confusion can't just be mine. You sit and play a home cartridge by yourself. Get where you can manage the affairs well enough to pull off a tolerably decent game in terms of objectives in the instruction booklet— clear the screen once in a while, protect your cities from missiles for twenty or so minutes, hold in there against those asteroids till you've got the overall space under control. It doesn't take long. Then stray from the official objectives and get a little into creating patterns as an end in its own right apart from "winning." You're likely to do that if you spend an evening alone with this confounded chip machine just lying around the house. And even if you've never "interacted" with a TV set but only bought the thing for the kids, get beyond any attitude you have about the blasted noisemakers and doodle with one of these little creatures for a while. Sit alone with your game, or select a cartridge from the kids' library that you can somehow stand, and you'll also ask what these silly creatures are really for, what potential they afford as engaging arenas for entertainment.

It looks like they're not even quite sure just how to market these home games. I noticed down the block that the Fotomat fast film developing chain now sells cartridges, perhaps inviting their aesthetic use. In Times Square down from the arcades, computers sit in discount display windows along with tiny TVs, portable one-person music systems, digital watches, miniature programmable piano keyboards, tiny high-efficiency shortwave radios and transmitters, and a plethora of other gadgets for individual and individualizing electronic involvement. Traditional boundaries are blurred to where you're not sure if you're adding numbers or making music, telling time or playing with bleeps, programming or being programmed. Will it all boil down to just so many different varieties of calculated doodling?

I paid thirty bucks for the thing, got my money's worth, can play a decent game of *Breakout*. But how do you sustain a single-minded competitive interest in these things when they hold a fascination far transcending the usual primary significance of a gaming field? By itself, a chess board, basketball court, Ping-Pong table, or racetrack in the solid world is nothing but a more or less bland setting for action. Sure golf courses can be handsomely groomed, the Le Mans Grand Prix traverses spectacular scenery, and there's the general tendency we have to embroider even the most instrumental activities with expressive flourish. But to the very extent aesthetic consideration is given to the design of a playing area, even when intended to increase competitive excitement, purely contextual features of play are embellished with other grounds for participation. Here we've got an extreme case, where the sheer novelty, colorfulness, and range of sights and sounds invite an interest in the object that enters into dialectic tension with its officially contrived purpose. Designed to make playing the game more engaging, these colorful little creatures under glass ask for experimental playfulness, particularly when you've got lots of free time around the house. And that undermines the competitive drive. If every time you bounced a basketball it made different sounds, you'd dribble more than necessary.

Moreover, the dribblable little creature is fundamentally set up for solitary use, and while turn taking can occur, the central "interaction" in this round of video games is between an individual user and the equipment. In light of that fact, motivating continued involvement becomes particularly problematic when whatever value a quarter has is no longer relevant and you're not inclined to try better because you're paying for your mistakes. Sitting by yourself, having already purchased all the action you could want, if you're not plugged into some social network—sociological jargon reflecting and preparing us for computer analysis—so that the announcement of your score and/or demonstration of your prowess is valued, there's a tendency to embellish the action in ways that make it self-motivating. Short of that, you'd put it away. Shoot baskets by yourself, put on a Sony Walkman and skate through the park, play a game of solitaire, and you drift into aesthetic elaborations—repetitions, colorations, free-form variations, improvisations of all sorts.

I'd likely throw the little quarterizer out the window at this point were it not for the triangles and quadrilaterals I've discovered, this way of playful pattern switching. Improvisational pattern play would seem to have guaranteed longevity, while best I can tell the optimum way to go uses itself up. At thirty bucks a throw that might be economically dangerous, but I for one would gladly pay more for a video setting with lots of challenging means to make up and manage moving forms and sounds. And working through a well-tempered progression of places with one of these regular shifting figures creates a recurring, nearly equidistant pulse that's elsewhere usually absent. A chance to get a bit more body into play.

I'll improvise along and create these patterns, forgetting the "ideal solution" with its constraints on free visual variation. Play with the forms instead. Sure *Breakout* is primitive compared with others even now on the market. But so are wooden recorders alongside Steinways or Moog synthesizers, and that doesn't stop us from making great music on them. As the engineer said, "*Breakout* plays well," and its very simplicity asks for further exploration. Direct descendant of the original *Pong*, its organizational elegance demands critical respect.

I've got a triangle moving across from right to left again, and at a certain point I manage to make a switching shift, shoot over to the far left side, and then get a similar shape coming back the other direction. But it feels like it's speeding up. I'm getting would tight, and the object is sucking me into its quarterizing mentality. It's nine thirty at night, midtown Manhattan was insanely frantic today, and the last thing I need at the moment is a carnivalized rush of adrenaline. The kids are back in California, I don't have to listen to New Wave rock full blast, so at least let me hold my bleeps and lights down to where their arrhythmicity doesn't wrench my nervous system into static.

Remember the manual said the ball speeds up after the twelfth return, and remember I said I usually get to the slam by that point anyhow? Well, now I'm laying low, thanks to the deflection shot that keeps me rising toward that slam. Come on, deflect already so I can get into a wide pattern that'll lead to my triangle; slow me down, computer, and then I'll hold you there as long as possible before I let you slam. You think you're keeping me from breaking out fast? Well, be my guest. I'm staying in a cross-screen pattern on the second and third bands at this interim pace between the slow lobbing ball and fast shot, the phase I always like most, when things gradually pick up just a bit and you've got a little smoothness going before the abrupt shift. Slow opening balls are real lazy, the distances always disparate one place to the next, so you hang in midair waiting shot by shot, drifting in a metrical vacuum of arithmetic space while the computer counts off number of a perfect monotone. And the slam is way up there, keeping you on your toes without letting you dance. But in between you've got a nice up-tempo stride that's good for pattern maintenance.

The slam shot is a distraction, for just as I was entering into another possible shape, one of them came along and put me out of commission. I'd forgotten all about it, forgotten about holding on to the action in general as I tried to sustain this geometric pattern in particular. And from out of nowhere, *whap*, I grab it with the corner of my eye, well enough to make the return and keep the ball in play. But I lose control of a traversing angular progression. And the pulse gets jacked right up to the two-bit thrill level.

The speed itself isn't the trouble. I can stay perfectly on top of a way upbeat pace at the piano without getting frazzled. The problem is that the regularity of the ball's movement between unequal distances produces articulations that are disjointedly placed, as we've seen. And as the speed increases quickly, coupled with these steadily moving lights, the body seems to be thrown off symmetrical balance into a sort of gestural aphasia. You get stuffed with mathematical indigestion. That's well and good for a spate of action in a night on the town, for a fast game before dinner to put in a little rah rah rah with the kids. But I'm trying to lie down and relax, so give me a break, cut out the slam shot, let me at least get in touch with the arrhythmia when it's a bit gentle and I can perhaps teach myself to feel its nature, to somehow even appreciatively seize hold of it. Give me the option, a rate-control knob, not like on some arcade games where the speed you select is tied to a score so unless you go fast you don't last long. Give me a thirty-dollar stay-at-home rate-control knob, so I can choose the values I want to compete for, so I can make the action more an end in its own right when I want, not just something to hold on to and get through with.

Of course I could slow things and take up one of those longer term adventure games, more fit to a relaxed night at home, where I leisurely stalk from maze to maze in search of some hidden goal. Or I could select from a variety of available microworlds to fill my evening with intensities that match the overall balance of frenzy and calm in a night's worth of TV. A little interview with the victim here, a few wrong leads there, a three-minute car chase when I've finally got the guy nailed down, and then a commercial where the last game's leftovers go through color changes to advertise itself. I could get caught right up in the seduction of the computer's capacity and major current use to offer rapid problem solving as the dominant motif for entertaining myself.

In fact it's already happening. I've found myself playing with the cursor on my word processor just for the hell of it, seeing if I could track it across screen and get it to stop at every comma in the text. I bought one of those calculator watches with a number game like the guys had in front of me on the plane. First there was problem solving to figure out how to use the thing. I'm walking up Madison Avenue, want to know what time it is so I can set my watch, and end up having to sit down for a half hour's worth of programmed instruction with a twenty-page booklet to figure out how. Then I'm walking along farther and go into stopwatch mode, counting steps to see if I can walk at precisely two per second. And to top it all off, I spent a full lunch hour in a classy restaurant playing the number whapping game, the watch off my wrist, squeezing these pinhead-sized buttons with two thumbs to match up and race digits across the display, working up a little sweat to reach a score of 4,350 that then stays in the memory of the thing like initials of high scorers on arcade games, so every time I look at the "game mode" I'm reminded of my Casio Bleeping Quotient. "He's got an IQ of 138, an SAT of 730, and a CBQ of 4,350." My latest total stays there on my wrist forever, like a tattoo. "Excuse me, sir, but may I see your high score?" Boy, am I going to get perfect.

I could take on new problems to solve, but I'd rather stay with *Breakout* for the while. It's a nice doodling machine, there's a simple formal elegance to the thing, its harmoniously balanced grid uncluttered by doodads and monsters, the tracing of the ball so light and airy. And with the increasingly finer sense of angles I'm developing, it invites the impulse for symmetrical music with well-formed figures moving rhythmically around. Then too there's something compelling about the very ways it jars me, about that melody-making failure, how it's so much like solid world action that clips right along, and yet so different. It's like one of the lemurs they make such a big deal out of in biology classes, lying at the border between two phyla and hence informative of the transformation that occurred on the threshold of a new mode of being. An "action game" helps keep alive the ambiguous experience of this mutated form of touch we now have between our mobile bodies and its calculating reflections, keeps the mysterious interface more accessible for our inspection, situates us precisely at that point where our hitherto natural mobile tendencies come into conflict with this number machine and the new ways of existing in these microworld sights and sounds.

Just make the pace under variable user control. And get rid of that band too for that matter, or at least let me have the option of moving it up to the top of the screen so it becomes a set of destinations and not an obstacle, and as I get higher up another band comes on, not jarring me, not faster and faster so I have to stay on top of excellence. It just comes on so I have a longer term arena for exploration, so I can play more or less gently for a half hour without gamey interruptions. I know. I'll just hit the reset button in reverse order for now. Whenever a pattern's maintenance is interrupted by a degree of rapidity that forces me to hold on to my quarter, I'll start again. Stay low and gentle. Whenever I get near the end and the finish tempts me to go for the kick, I'll stop. I don't want to break through, don't want to near the end and be drawn into the contest despite myself, to get all worked up because I've missed a shot. As soon as a slam comes I get into the intensity again, and then unless I control the barricade's destruction in a strategically sound way to avoid the development of holes, I'm back up against those frantically shifting rectangles that are impossible to consistently manage unless your life depends on winning. The slam speed creates the thrill of the game at the same time as it begs you to discover a strategic way to get around having to go crazy. And without the constraint of a contest or limited quarters, I'd fall right back into my five-shot opening again, God forbid.

I turn the sounds off now and sit up close, two feet from the TV, the room pitch-black. I serve. The ball comes down. Watch it float, as in thin liquid, thrustless and constant. I follow it down and bring the paddle into place, so to speak, hardly doing much "bringing," rather making a friction less decision in which the hand's involvement feels quite fortuitous. And I go "bump" to myself, in the back of my head somewhere. As it goes through its checklisting paces I can't help but accompany each point of feigned articulation with an inner saying. It "hits" a brick and I silently hum a bump to myself, then the side wall, bump, and the paddle again, bump. The sounds are off so I supply them myself, old-fashioned solid person that I am, unable to transcend some way of feeling myself connected to the task by at least doing something I can tactilely appreciate so I'll know I'm really here, and not merely a nonbeing the TV set uses to complete an electronic circuit so its programmed balls stay in motion. Geneticists have gotten where they define human beings as DNA's way of making more DNA, an update of the notion a chicken is the way one egg makes another. Now, as computers are being programmed to do programs, there emerges the prospect that our vital function is as button pushers keeping software in operation. I say bump to myself, not that it matters, not that it helps. Just so I can feel something.

I've put the sounds back on full blast, and have a sequence of adjacent bricks moving cross the bottom two rows again. A couplet of distances between paddle and bricks repeats itself precisely as the same form shifts over a notch at a time, the bleeps spaced with a pulsing regularity that's accessible to my tapping foot:

… bleep beep … bleep beep … bleep beep … bleep beep …

Well, I've finally got a rhythm I can grasp, by God, a chance to dribble the thing after all, the only evenness I've yet to find in the game. And at this and only this very point could it be said the object has been incorporated as an instrumental extension of the body. I'm going somewhere, knowing I'll get right to that next particular adjacent brick and knowing just when I'll get there. I don't have to wait for the time of arrival as the ball floats along of its own clocked accord as my eyes are just led in anticipation. Instead, the established pulse is extended toward the next target and I aim for a known place and time up ahead, taking charge of the action with a melodic gesture in full command of itself.

So it went, for an hour or so, hitting the reset button when things got too hectic, searching for these equidistant setups that'd bring me in sync with the bleeps, playing my instrument, finally bringing the creature under control. And it was fun enough to watch these little patterns of adjacent bricks metrically popping off, aiming for this and then that particular spot and getting here and then there right on anticipated time, incorporating the object as an extension of my gestural will. The sounds could stand improvement, but that's a trivial complaint, nothing a little technology can't solve, already has solved for other games. A full widescreen TV with more saturated colors would be nice too.

Then at one point I got into a lockup. A hole was created so the ball went through a nearly rectangular full-court pattern without hitting anything. I just stayed there for maybe a full five minutes, not moving the paddle, going over and over and over through the same points until I'd grasped its slightly syncopated pulse. I took my hand off the knob, careful not to disturb the shape, sat back with all the home relaxation you could ask for, played my picture music, and had a good laugh.

Well, it's under control now, that's for sure. The program is doing what I want, its time and places possessed under my strict management, the switching instrument playing the song I've chosen, *bleep … bleep … bleep … bleep … bleep … bleep.* And look Ma, no hands. But what more could you say I'm doing when this knob sits in my palm like a box of popcorn as triangular figures cross the picture screen in a regular pulsing sequence? Sure the bleeps are metrical and gentle, and I can tap along with them. But who am I kidding? I'm not hitting anything, just flicking switches. I've set up a pattern, and the ball is directed to the right successive spots through minuscule paddle shifts organized by some subtactile, neurological mechanisms that can stay in efficient and precise operation behind the most disinterested sort of vacant gaze at the screen. For all intensive purposes I'm appreciating the action nearly exclusively as a witness, and if I sway a little with the ball, tap with the bleeps, or even move my arms back and forth a bit as the shots proceed, this deceptive way of feeling engaged in performing rather quickly experiences its own meagerness. There's no heft in the paddle whatever. My hand goes through its movements without any sense of an impact on things, nothing feels managed, nothing grasped. The hand is motivationally limp, while the kick of doing these sequences only resides in that little pride you take in precisely seeing the angled course as your hand tags along to fulfill the eyes' hope. The fun is watching the orderly progression, such as it is. But as for the bodily experience of making such patterns? The ongoing creation of this picture music as an engaging melodic gesture in its own right? Barely touches doodling, tactilely pale by comparison.

Then something altogether mind blowing knocked the phenomenological wind right out of me. I did what they told me good players could do.

I had been switching a triangle across the bottom two rows, then got into another pattern that wasn't quite metrical but close enough to bend with a little anyhow. The slam came and I said what the heck, why not try to rhythmically seize it too? So I played out a little equidistant pulsable run with it for a while, and before I knew it I noticed I was way down to about four of five bricks when I missed a return. Why not clear the screen for old computer times' sake? There they were again, those little sneaky leftovers. So I served and got right into a lockup, which usually happens when there's little on screen, and I stayed doodling with the fixed trapezoid for a few rounds and then managed to scoot it over and hit a fast slam brick that threw me off retinal balance and I missed. I served the third ball right into another frozen shape, the tricky sort to move over because it nailed my eyes into the corner on a tiny little rebound angle where it's hard for them to think. But I managed it, scooted the next figure over a couple of notches, and cleared the screen. The field now was dark for a second.

Then flash, the full six-band July 4th technicolor barricade suddenly popped right back on the screen so you could start off from scratch with the ball still in motion, a dazzling dare to "do me again," lighting my face, switching on the want. What in the world was that? In the clock-ticking option I'd always played, you don't get a new screen if you clear one off. But in the version where points are tallied for bricks, if you go all the way a full new barricade flashes right on and you can stay in continuous action with a fresh supply of bricks. Paul told me on the telephone that he'd discovered that one day, but it had no relevance for me since I was into this one screen clearing goal. But for some reason the machine happened to be set on this scoring option that night, and it was the first time I'd ever cleared the screen in that mode.

Hey, I want that new stage again. The regenerated barricade perked me right up like the curtain rising on your favorite Broadway musical, the full micro fix took hold with a bolt that sucked my synapses back up to how it was on that shootout at the interface with my first last brick. Well, I came down on that reset button with all juices pumping, going full steam ahead. How many barricades can I clear? Luckily I got a corner serve, though the caring was high enough up there that to tell the truth I probably could've done just as well with a center one. I went through some new slight variation on my five shot opening that worked to nonetheless get to the slam brick on time. And I watched it ready to hit, picked it right up and headed for the top, knowing however that I wasn't gonna slice through with this configuration. The opening wedge can almost look right, but sometimes a brick is in the way that'll give you a return you can't send back.

You get where you anticipate troubles like this, And when you're really into holding on, a strongly caring look quite suddenly brings that vague invisible grid of angles and lines into a familiar neighborhood of well-marked roadways. So instead of waiting for this return, since I knew handling it gets pretty tight, I switched over to the other side and got into a little cross-screen pattern there for a while, a double band fast couplet I could move right to left. Then I switched it back, this time from an angle that would carry me through, and I broke out, getting a quick gasping breath of relief as the ball bounced up on top. And I used the short pause to tell myself: care.

I can't say for sure why I decided to care more this time. Macho pride. Pent-up frustration. Man over machine. I don't really know why I said care and keep caring. Whenever the focal plane got the least bit dreamy, whenever my look seemed to start losing its want, and then to just throw in lots of them for continuing protection, I said, "care," "care," "care." Said it inside. Said it with my eyes. Can't really say why. Just made the decision to stay with the ball, to stick myself right inside it, to forget about swaying and just switch myself on to the moving geometry and bleepy collisions, metrical or not. Don't fight it, just count it, putting the old musical movements on hold if need be. When it's 4/4 time, tap if you like, when it's 7/4.51, just freeze.

Someday maybe we'll get to tap to that too. We'll feel our retinas tapping.

The fresh new goal had its familiar way of pulling me right into a good rush of caring, and this time it just happened, that's the best I can say, that I made that sort of a commitment you know you're going to keep. Maybe it's a pathetic symptom of some modern malaise in a world lacking things really worth striving for, that could get a guy alone in his hotel room to put his will on the Atari sort of line. Perhaps the game is a pure place to get yourself a good spate of solitary willpower in a social world with decreasing options for courageous expression. Then too maybe it was the twenty minutes of a *Kojak* rerun I watched a half hour before. How do I know why I said this time I'm going to make it, with nobody there, not the least interest in telling anyone, no thought of the months of investment, nothing but existence at stake. Holding on. I don't know why I decided to go all the way, but here's how I did it.

For one thing, I sure could see those angles now, each and every one of them. The bands were there to be removed, pure and simple, no two ways about it. I pitched the ball back up top two more times through the customary slice you're supposed to use. But the barricade was looking messy over near the other side, so instead of pitching up top again and leaving that untidiness to make for trouble later, I planned a switchover to clean things up a bit over there. I wasn't sure exactly what

I'd do once I got there, what sort of cleanup it would allow when it came down to details. To my glance it just looked like a brick wall about to cave in. But I figured that if I got over there and could take away some of the odd pieces and square things up a bit, my distances and shapes wouldn't get too crazy later on. I switched over, not knowing just which one I'd hit, but I got one stray brick out of the picture, hooked my look right onto the path it would then follow and spotted just those bricks the next shots could hit. And then when I managed to put things back into the more or less rectangular shape I figured would help me out later, I switched back again to the breakthrough slice and stayed up top for a couple more runs.

Another quick breath as it bounced along on top, thankfully giving me a second with nothing to do. Now I saw that there'd soon be a hole on the far right, had to watch out for returns from both sides. And as it got down to the end like this I had some feelings in my hand. I centered myself in midcourt, and squeezed the paddle a little. I squeezed it to feel my hand squeezing. I could feel myself move it a tiny touch over, to prepare for shots this side or that. I probably didn't have to squeeze it. But I did. It was a caring squeeze.

When I got into a lockup at the end a short while later, my hand made it feel itself further. It was a long diagonal one

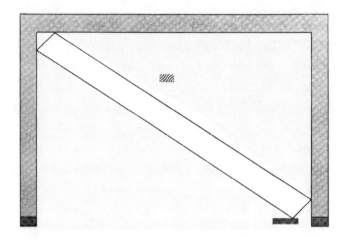

with the ball going fast. And now the very last brick was right nearby. I held the figure there for a while. Take a few breaths, forget about the bleeps, let the body recover from its siege of catatonic repression but don't tap your foot because you never know what numbers are coming up. Hold still. And I held still, watching that lockup, fading away for a few coordinates here and there, saying, "Come on and care." Fighting that hypnotizing pattern, I began to tickle the paddle between shots, real quickly and very minutely every time the ball was up top. I tried out the tiniest little wiggles till my fingers could feel the distance between real close coordinates, getting set for a nudge toward that brick. In the interface at last, handling the care, I felt my hand feel that it knew where to go, and then, pop, it was over.

REMEMBRANCE

PAUL'S BIGGEST ANXIETY ABOUT coming to Manhattan for the summer was whether or not he'd be able to get on a Little League team. I told him I couldn't guarantee that in particular, but as soon as I finished up some work in a couple of days I'd help him find an athletic program of one sort or another. No sooner had he gotten in from Kennedy than he discovered one great thing about being in New York was the extensive baseball coverage on cable TV. Spotting him posing before the set, mimicking batting stances and pitching styles, I remembered myself as a kid fencing down the block on the way home from Errol Flynn movies on Saturday afternoons, jumping fire hydrants, every alley a secret castle corridor, every puddle a moat.

One evening around ten thirty, I went into his bedroom in the sublet we'd rented and sat down to watch a game with him.

"Where's it coming from, LA?"

"No, it's the Yankee Stadium."

"A rerun?" I asked.

"It's a night game, dummy."

The way your own kids talk to you these days.

Across the street from the Stadium, where I grew up, you knew when there was a night game because the whole sky was lit for blocks around, and in the stands there was a very special excitement in how the artificial blazing light streamed down to create what seemed like a fantasy land, a county fair, summertime in one of its mystical transformations. What a joy a night game was for a little kid, to feel the magic of those giant bulbs, the brilliance of July in shirt sleeves with no sweat, a sudden transportation to some glorious gathering of athletes in a country field. On TV you know it's a night game by looking at your calendar/date/time-zone wristwatch. With sports coverage using theatrical framing techniques, long shots taking in sky and lights reserved for the end of the show when the crowd dispersed, feelings of the season and hour were annihilated. There was just this tight shot of the diamond with a synthetic bright midsummer's day green, Alabama clay dirt, gleaming white starched uniforms, and the air conditioning in your own room. You didn't notice the lack of shadows. As I looked back and forth between this live broadcast daylight eight miles north and the darkness out the window on the Upper East Side, for a moment I felt a bit confused, like the guy at the Berkeley party who rocked back and forth in his chair with the *Breakout* paddle. Shows how out of touch I'd been, or in touch, depending on how you see things.

He wanted to play for real, however, was getting impatient to find a team, and when he got into trouble with the information operator on the phone one morning, "Hey Dad, what 'borough' do I want?" I told him to bring me the Yellow Pages.

He hung on my shoulder as I leafed through it, detouring here and there to illustrate a little rundown on how extraordinary Manhattan was. Look at all these pages after pages only for doctors, or for lawyers, even answering services. In a few minutes he interrupted, "Why don't we put it on the computer?"

I'd bought mine for word processing, that new way of doing thinking. Speaking of green, a strange thing had happened. When I first got it, whenever I put in more than a half hour at the console, I'd leave the avocado and black screen and everything around me had a pinkish tinge for about twenty minutes. Papers, the numerals on the telephone dial, the sky-line out the window, all cast light rosy. I'd asked people about it, nobody with a computer corroborated the experience, and I worried about that afterglow for a while until a friend said something about oversaturation, about red and green as complementary colors. Sounded reasonable. Besides, it then went away. In about two weeks I suppose my eyes "adjusted," whatever that means. They take more green without an overload? I don't know exactly how it goes, does anyone, really? Do I now see green less vividly? Might Paul, after years of sitting three feet away from TV grass? I'd trade in the PC for an old-fashioned chipless self-correcting model in a minute, no matter how quickly I can store, retrieve, insert, block move, delete, reform, and the rest, if it's going to make summer look different. Or will I? Carbon monoxide must have smelled horrible during the first days of the Model T. Then we forgot about it, for the most part still have. Nostrils toughen up. Retinas too, I suppose.

I had the computer, though going anywhere beyond word processing with it was a complete mystery to me. I hadn't the slightest idea what the mechanics of programming involved. But I knew I could've told him you didn't just "put" things on the computer, that at least for now you or some other humans had to first do all the work to get the machine ready for a project, that that'd be a complex job for even the simple search procedure we wanted. Yet there was a touch of the software entrepreneur in his tone, and maybe he knew all about the complexities anyhow, wasn't at all actually suggesting a way to handle our particular problem of the moment. Kids have a way of forecasting.

So say you solve all of the difficulties and put the "resources" on the computer, simultaneously reconstructing the world's facilities so they become networkable. And now, instead of letting the fingers do the walking, you save them most of the effort by having just the tip of one do the thinking about where to get what you want. You don't stroll anymore, browsing about. You poke at options. Window-shopping Yellow Page fingers learn the computer goosestep.

Kids don't seem to be much into strolling anyhow these days. When we went shopping later that afternoon in a large sporting goods store to find a batter's glove, whatever that is, Paul couldn't find one and didn't understand why in the world I kept resisting asking a salesperson. He didn't see the point in insisting for yourself that you find something on your own by browsing around, not wanting to make it go fast, at times even purposefully taking a roundabout route to where you think it might be because you enjoy that kind of navigating.

I guess I'm just old-fashioned. Take the word processor for instance. Every once in a while I miss my old IBM electric. Now and then I find myself gently running the balls of my fingers over lines of text, touching the TV screen as I read, not pointing to avoid losing place but to feel the rhythms of the voice, handle the sentences, supplement the meter of inner speech with another tactile dimension by tracing unfolding phrases with a caress that further evokes the texture and palpable pulse of the sounds. I miss the looks and feel of a good bond paper, the crisp impression of the letters, that very slight but significant third dimension, the inkedness of it all. I used to love putting a half-dozen sheets in the carriage at the same time to make the type really black and heavy, especially on a final draft. I miss the loudness.

I probably do printouts too often, thumbing my nose at some aspects of the device's efficiency, writing what I guess is a few pages and then quickly running off actual ones to leaf through, not yet thoroughly acclimated to button reading, confused at times by the current cultural lag that requires I scroll through a continuous stream of sights while nonetheless reading on behalf of others who'll handle paginated ones. How can I fully know how a certain discussion feels without holding it in my hands, dreamily or impatiently fingering back and forth to assess rhythm and flow, find times for a pause, shift in tempo or meter, a splice, flashback, close-up. I can't yet scroll on behalf of other scrollers, haven't done enough fingertip reading, and there's an arrhythmic edge to the passage of paragraphs, an anxiety about the compositional aphasia I might encounter with these instantaneously reassembling sheets of electrical talk that will still have to make their way onto paper. I do more printouts than the whole setup is intended for so I can page my way through a reading and handle the pacing of the talk. And besides, I can then take a draft outside, to a cafe, and edit in the midst of the world, if I'm lucky enough to put myself in one of those increasingly hard-to-find but wonderful little communities of writers who sit at tables and never speak and yet feel somehow engaged in a collective mission by their very copresence out there in the town together.

There's one experience in particular at the word processor that gets me downright angry at times. There's no more of that room for finger breathing while you awaited a carriage's return. You reach the end of a processed line of text and if your word becomes too long for the margin while there's still allotted space to get it underway, it splits in the midst of your articulation and your voice instantaneously reappears six inches to the left, a quarter of an inch lower. The computer can't know what you're about to write, not yet, not a word or even a letter in advance, has to wait and merely calculate how things are going in order to then "decide" where to put the sound.

Before, you felt a big word welling up, hit the carriage return, lifted off from the keyboard just a bit, reorganized your grasp, and dug back into the improvisation with a renewed rhythmic mobilization to continue. And some of the things you found to say, you found because you said them that way. But now a nervous mathematical tic has entered your body and voice, a little electrical scratch chipped into your own internal thoughts to control the metric of your song. I get old-fashioned and insecure about the eerie implications of this speech numbering machine, unsure how to cope with or even detect the most thoroughgoing and mysterious transformations of finger speaking and its products it'll surely bring. So there are those special times where the way I want and need to feel myself think is nostalgic, for carriage returns, even pencils.

I got nostalgic at the Yellow Pages. Instead of moving in the suggested direction down from fingers to fingertip, I ended up putting even it aside and getting out onto the street, browsing in remembrance for a good old-fashioned beat cop to give me a hand on how to keep a fourteen year old out of trouble in the summer. I was thinking how midtown Manhattan was a far cry from Little Leaguesville, how I wasn't about to have him just check out those concrete battlefields that pass as schoolyards, how the only grass I knew about in the whole city was Central Park and that hardly brought to mind mothers in station wagons. Thinking that, the fingers half awake and half sleepwalking through "Associations and Organizations," I thought of "Athletic" and remembered. A storefront in the Bronx. I think the insignia on the window was green. I'd gone there at about age ten and taken up boxing for two weeks until it got the best of me. Mostly I think I'd joined to get a membership card and little button. PAL, the Police Athletic League, a youth organization with community precincts in neighborhoods throughout the five boroughs, where nice old semi-retired Irish cops who liked kids made sure nobody got hurt too bad and organized various outings and sports events. Perhaps it wasn't the sort of institution that a mass market network would likely access for middle-class users, but surely a socially sophisticated computer service could present such ethnically and racially mixed options for parents who cared that their kids had a range of social experiences. But be that as it may, it wasn't "information" about such a place that I counted on as I dialed for their local number, not at all. It was the recollection, of a world through which I'd browsed for years, a remembrance rich with images: cops who overlooked turned-on fire hydrants that served as our rivers, candy stores in summer where the best thing was the light until eight thirty so you could rush out right after dinner instead of sitting around with everyone listening to the radio, a good twenty varieties of games to play with a ball, some sidewalk cracks, and a stoop or two. When Joe DiMaggio walked through the streets and got spotted, kids came out of the concrete to follow this idol heading toward the Stadium on his way to work. And we didn't have the overriding impression that's nowadays the most striking feature you notice when seeing someone famous, that relatively new aspect of personal appearance that literally defines what fame has come to mean: roundedness. You spotted Joe DiMaggio and didn't say, "My God, there he is in three dimensions." You said, "There he is close up."

Whatever the PAL might be worth as a solution these days, I trusted it for starters at least, not because it was on some network, but because it was a piece of knowledge in the lived past. A flood of impressions crystallized around an image of that storefront, together making up that old-fashioned stock of knowledge about the social structure that we humans count on for deciding how to act.

Okay, don't show me the sky beyond Yankee Stadium, ABC, so I can spot the building I grew up in. Just don't narrow in on everything for heaven's sake, so I can only tell it's nighttime by my watch. But if it gets that bad, and we are to sit in front of consoles during most of the days to come, accessing information, at the very least give us user controllable rate knobs, Atari, make sure the interface stays flexible. Put it on the computer, but just make sure there's enough for your everyday user to do, so that participation in the culture's knowledge doesn't all reduce to discovering the optimum solution. At least make it so this generation of kids can complain to theirs in turn:

> Go out and buy the software for you, are you crazy? Get in your room and write it yourself, so you'll know you came up with something on the tip of your finger, and didn't just sit and wait for it to be retrieved.

The PAL turned out not to work after all, didn't fit his needs, and a friend suggested a baseball camp in Connecticut where he could stay for a week at a time and get lots of exercise and fresh air. He was delighted. As I put him and a duffel bag full of bats, mitts, yes, a batter's glove, and more on the train, he asked:

"Can I have an extra ten bucks a week?"

"Ten bucks? For what?"

"It says in the brochure they've got a video game room."

•

Coming back uptown from Grand Central Station, I had this fantasy. After a day of baseball practice, a late afternoon review of his progress on the videotape facilities the camp circular had advertised, and a two-hour after-dinner battle against missiles, Paul is walking from the video game room across a field toward the dormitory. It's muggy but cooling off. The dampness of the Sound is blowing in from the Connecticut shore. And he sees these little transistors flying around. Every so often, off there in the woods, a small light goes on for a second or two, moves about three feet, and goes dark. Now and then a real close one scares the pants off him.

ACKNOWLEDGMENTS

NUMEROUS PEOPLE FACILITATED the conduct of this research and preparation of the book. First I'd like to thank Alan Kaye and George Kiss of Atari, Inc., who afforded me access to their facilities and enabled me to engage programmers in conversations that proved invaluable to my project. I'm grateful for the cooperation, as well as for the assistance of Brad Stewart, formerly of Atari and now of the video firm IMAGIC, who kindly met with me at length to discuss the programming of *Breakout*.

Conversations with Harold Garfinkel and Manny Schegloff of UCLA, and Bert Dreyfus at Berkeley, were most helpful in the early stages of my investigation. Robert Epstein of New York read and reread the manuscript in its entirety and made deeply insightful suggestions at each turn. The book would have profited still more had I the capacity to incorporate his fine recommendations more thoroughly.

Special thanks are due to Claire Canning, who served as a jack-of-all-trades: helping with household responsibilities, working as a secretary, tutoring children, offering encouragement at every point. The project couldn't have been brought to completion without her extraordinary competence.

And last, but hardly least, I'm indebted to my children and parents for their support, patience and love.

David Sudnow, 1983

EDITOR'S
ACKNOWLEDGMENTS

Boss Fight Books would first and foremost like to thank Wendy Lu for entrusting us with her late husband's work and making this rerelease possible. Thank you also to Brendan Keogh for the tip, and to Jon Irwin, Anna Anthropy, and Keogh again for their insightful writings on *Pilgrim*. I'd also like to thank our awesome team for getting this book back into publication shape and helping make this the book's best edition yet: editor Michael P. Williams, copyeditor Ryan Plummer, proofreaders Nick Sweeney and Joe M. Owens, layout designer Christopher Moyer, and cover designer Cory Schmitz.

Gabe Durham

ALSO FROM
BOSS FIGHT BOOKS